THE BOY WITH THE THORN IN HIS SIDE

THE BOY WITH
THE THORN IN HIS SIDE

A MEMOIR

KEITH FLEMING

 Perennial

An Imprint of HarperCollins*Publishers*

A hardcover edition of this book was published in 2000 by William Morrow, an imprint of HarperCollins Publishers.

HarperCollins books may be purchased for educational, business, or sales promotional use. For information please write: Special Markets Department, HarperCollins Publishers Inc., 10 East 53rd Street, New York, NY 10022.

First Perennial edition published 2001.

Designed by Oksana Kushnir

The Library of Congress has catalogued the hardcover edition as follows:

Fleming, Keith.
    The boy with the thorn in his side: a memoir / Keith Fleming—1st ed.
        p. cm.
    ISBN 0-688-16839-6
    1. White, Edmund, 1940– —Family. 2. Authors, American—20th century—Family relationships. 3. Gay men.—United States—Family relationships. 4. Young men—New York (State)—New York—Biography. 5. Uncles—New York (State)—New York—Biography. 6. Fleming, Keith. I. Title.

PS3573.H463 Z68 2000
813'.54—dc21
[B]
                                                      99-055718

ISBN 0-06-095930-4 (pbk.)

01 02 03 04 05 BP 10 9 8 7 6 5 4 3 2 1

FOR MARI AND MURDOCH

ACKNOWLEDGMENTS

I'd like to thank Will Schwalbe for his kind encouragement and suggestions at the very beginning; my agent, Charlotte Sheedy, and my editors, Paul Bresnick and Ben Schafer, for their belief in me and the book; and my mother, my sister, my Uncle Ed, and my friends Donny, Laura, and Pat for their openhearted help in remembering our past. And I especially want to thank my friend Bryan for all his help.

CONTENTS

PROLOGUE   1

CHAPTER 1: The Flemings and the Whites   5

CHAPTER 2: Mom and the Free School   37

CHAPTER 3: The Horrors to Come   62

CHAPTER 4: Dr. Schwarz and Laura   81

CHAPTER 5: Life with Uncle Ed   108

CHAPTER 6: Playing House   147

CHAPTER 7: Back in the Provinces   184

The boy with the thorn in his side ... behind
the hatred there lies a plundering desire ... for love.

—"The Boy with the Thorn in His Side," The Smiths

THE BOY WITH THE THORN IN HIS SIDE

To look at the picture, you'd think he was the father. He stands there smiling, leaning protectively over my mother and me. The poem he's just written about my birth also sounds like a father's:

Did we live right then, when your mother and I were
   young?
We had no way of knowing.
But as a woman comes to know the judgment of her
   deeds
by the signs left on her face seen in a mirror
Years later,
So we shall see the end of all our moments
impressed upon your still-soft bones.

Though he would become a sort of father to me—more than a father—he's in fact my mother's younger brother, the novelist Edmund White. The poem is called "To His Nephew," and its prediction turned out to be right: years later, when I became a troubled teenager, my uncle saw my condition as somehow forming a "judgment" on his and my mother's haunted past. In 1976, at the worst moment of my adolescence, he came to my rescue by bringing me to live with him in New York. It was the defining moment of my life because it saved me from the horrible fate my real father had mapped out for me. Under my uncle's distinctive influence I became a new and better person.

But no one would have taken my uncle for a father figure when I lived with him then. Because if he'd been a curiously old-looking college student when he wrote "To His Nephew"—a geeky, bespectacled 1950s intellectual who wore the drab slacks and jackets his father ordered up from his Cincinnati tailor—by the time I went to live with him my uncle looked barely older than I did. He was in his mid-thirties by then but with his cherubic, unlined face and leather bomber jacket, my uncle and his unending energy had made me feel like the old one as I watched him fielding his nonstop telephone calls and heading out the door each night to prowl his favorite downtown bars.

Today I'm nearly forty and my uncle nearly sixty and these days he looks like a real father figure. There's silver in his hair, jowls on his face, and many more pounds of flesh on his frame. Except I don't see him as a father anymore, nor would he want me to. Just the other day he was complaining that a young friend had blurted out to him, "You're my father figure, Ed"—something my uncle so hated hearing that he immediately told the young man, "Oh. Well, you're *my* father figure."

No, these days my uncle is more like a venerable, funny friend of mine—someone I laugh with on the phone. And yet there was a strange evening not too long ago when I found myself suddenly feeling almost like his mother. My uncle had come to Providence, Rhode Island, where I live, to give a lecture at Brown University's French department. His lecture, as he told his audience with his disarming little-boy smile, was entitled "Literary Lesbianism." He'd just dashed the thing off that very afternoon on the train from New York. A few months earlier my uncle had published a short biography of Proust, and "Literary Lesbianism" delved into some ingenious transpositions Proust had worked into *Remembrance of Things Past*. Apparently one of Proust's problems had been how to give Marcel, his heterosexual stand-in, something approximating the pathos Proust himself knew in his love life as a gay man often attracted to straight men. The solution? An entirely literary lesbianism. For Proust transformed his own heterosexual male loves into the young lesbian characters who haunt Marcel—lesbians, as my uncle pointed out to us, in whom we can detect a certain odd, exuberant boyishness.

After the lecture I ducked out for a quick cigarette in the cobbled courtyard and was disturbed to see dozens and dozens of crows noisily roosting in the overhanging trees. It seemed like a bad omen of something.

The next day my uncle, now back in New York, called me up with some horrible news: he'd suffered a "little stroke" on the train back from Providence. At least that's what he thought had happened. He'd be going in for tests the next day but his doctor was already alarmed about possible brain damage. "I was sitting there talking to the friend who was riding with me, when suddenly I stopped making sense," my uncle told me. "For a full minute I was just babbling nonsense, apparently. Then it felt like somebody injected me with novocaine—my whole body went numb with pins and needles. My face, my lips, became paralyzed for a bit and I started drooling."

It was so characteristic of my uncle to tell me this only several minutes into our phone call. Instead of immediately exclaiming, "God, guess what? I think I had a stroke this morning," his opening words were: "You know, I'm so stupid. When I got home today I realized I forgot to include the disk to that CD I gave your girlfriend last night." He asked if I'd enjoyed the evening and I said I'd loved "Literary Lesbianism" and appreciated

how attentive he'd been to my girlfriend at the reception afterward (at one point my uncle had actually squatted down next to
where she was sitting, the small bald spot at the crown of his
head suddenly visible, in order to give her his most respectful
and undivided attention).

Not until I asked how the evening had been for him did he
finally get around to telling me about his stroke. He was washing
dishes in his kitchen now, I could hear, and only because I knew
what had happened could I detect in his voice the faintest fra-
gility, a slightly more careful way of speaking than his usual
silvery flow. But the biggest sign that this was an extraordinary
occasion was how he kept lingering on the phone with me. Ordinarily my uncle was brisk and purposeful, signing off at the
first hint of a lull if not before. I could take it for granted that
I was only one of maybe thirty phone calls he'd be packing into
his hectic day. His mother, my grandmother Delilah, had been
fond of saying he deliberately "overbooked" his life; that what
most people would find overwhelming was for him merely the
daily feeding of an enormous appetite for social stimulation.
She'd loved recalling the dinner for ten he once gave where at
one point he was simultaneously on the phone, cooking at the
stove, pouring out wine, and greeting arriving guests at the door.

But now, this night, my uncle seemed to draw real comfort
from just staying on the line with me. As our call crept past the
one-hour mark it hit me that were his mother still alive it would
probably be she he'd be warming himself in cozy chitchat with
on the phone as he tried to steady his nerves. It touched me that
with her death I'd become the person he thought to turn to at
this dark moment.

Though his doctor eventually decided he hadn't suffered a
stroke at all but just a weirdly intense allergic reaction, I'll always
remember that long phone call with my uncle when everything
was still so uncertain and when the tears had sprung to my eyes
at one point because it moved me to think that I could be of
any help to him. I owe him so much, after all.

THE FLEMINGS AND THE WHITES

My mother says she married Daddy for his mother, for his family. My father had grown up on a chicken farm outside Cleveland as one of a crewcut brood of brothers and it was the very averageness of Dad's family, the Fleming clan, that attracted my mother. The Flemings were a breath of fresh air; all-American, unassuming, and simple—everything Mom's own small, splintered family, the Whites, was not. Dad's mother, my Grandma Fleming, had been starstruck by Mom from the time Dad first started bringing her home from college for weekends at the family farmhouse. Grandma Fleming would sit with Mom for hours in the dark cellar "candling" eggs—holding each freshly hatched egg over a candle flame to see if it was marred by a bloody fertilized spot.

Grandma Fleming found in Mom the woman friend

she'd always wanted, while Mom found in her the mother she'd been looking for. Unlike Mom's actual mother, Delilah White, Grandma Fleming was a married homemaker who exuded a cozy calm that, particularly when Mom was around, became attentive and admiring. Grandma Fleming's presence—so decent, like a country morning—gave Mom the soothing sense that she herself was at last becoming normal and escaping the influence of what she regarded as her own "weirdo" family. Mom's parents had divorced when she was ten and after that it had been all downhill. Her mother, Delilah, never really recovered from her divorce and became tearful, heavy-drinking, and melodramatic, sometimes even threatening to jump out the window of their luxury hotel suite or to drive them all into Lake Michigan in her Cadillac. Meanwhile Mom's father, E.V., a wealthy businessman, had settled into a second marriage with his secretary—a woman who soon enough was acting the part of wicked stepmother, nearly strangling twelve-year-old Mom with a telephone cord once during an argument.

Growing up like this my mother came to associate affluence and culture with misery and isolation, even with perversity. Her father had once cruelly shown her her "life bill," a methodical accounting of every last cent he'd ever spent on her. More shocking, at the very time Mom began taking refuge at my father's family's chicken farm for long weekends in the mid-1950s, Mom's younger brother, my Uncle Eddie, horrified the family by announcing that he was so afflicted with homosexuality he needed long-term psychoanalysis in order to be cured. Eddie had already been making Mom's miserable adolescence even worse for years by getting so bound up with their mother that Mom always felt like a third wheel. Delilah's worship of her son was so sickeningly flagrant, in fact, that she declared more than once that for her "God is number one and Ed is number two." Though my mother never disputed that her little brother was clearly some kind of genius, she saw little good in it. If anything, she resented how often Eddie had embarrassed her over the years in front of her friends, holing himself up in his room with opera records that were audible throughout the house, emerging now and then in his horn-rim glasses to tell everyone about his harp and tap dancing lessons, or about how he could no longer eat meat because he'd become a Buddhist. Now to top it all off, Eddie had come down with this terrible, terribly embarrassing illness, homosexuality.

And so in the crowded but very normal Fleming farmhouse, my mother had finally found a world she liked as well as a stage on which she could shine.

I tell you all this because by the time I myself was a teenager it became more and more mysterious to me that Mom had ever married Dad. Practically from the day my parents' divorce went through (April Fool's Day, 1971), my mother started mocking my now-absent father. She'd mimic the way he would invariably say, "Well, let me think about it," in response to any and all requests, even the most minor ("Can I have another Coke, Dad?"). But my mother's imitation of Dad exaggerated his flat voice, making it stubbornly, woodenly stupid. As Mom played him, my father became a cross between a robot and a retarded person. But my mother's favorite put-down of Dad was actually an observation that Uncle Eddie had once shared with her privately—that my father was "like a long freight train where every car is exactly the same."

What my mother failed to tell me then was that my father's charm for her had always resided in how plainly he adored her, how he made her feel like a real prize. He was in fact the only boy she'd ever really dated. As a girl Mom had been so uncomfortable around boys that she developed what amounted to two different personalities. During the school year she was shy and awkward, a dowdy girl a bit overweight in her long tartan skirt. But each July, when she went off to an all-girl summer camp in Rhinelander, Wisconsin, the dowdiness would melt from her along with the pounds as her hair turned platinum in the sun, her skin deep brown, and she changed into a powerful, magnetic leader of the other girls. It was not until she went off to college that she finally found in my father a boy as unintimidating as an old shoe, someone she could dazzle and dominate. Mom and Dad started dating as sophomores and by junior year they had become engaged—two twenty-year-olds already so domesticated that they spent their dates fantasizing about the family they would raise.

By the mid-1960s Mom and Dad were raising us, their family of three kids, in a small white house in the leafy old Chicago suburb of Evanston. My father was now the principal of an elementary school in nearby Skokie. And my mother, just as she'd seen Dad's mother, Grandma Fleming, do, threw herself into being a homemaker, working her way through mountains of ironing each day. I still marvel at how well laundered we all look in family pictures throughout the sixties, the crisp white shirts, the spiffy cardigans with shiny buttons. And we didn't just look this way on special picture-taking occasions; we were neatly outfitted nearly all the time. In one of my favorite family pictures my mother, looking wonderfully young with her pale, pretty, unlined face, her blonde hair swept up in a neat bun, is sitting cross-legged on the living room rug holding a classical guitar. My little sister Susie and I are nestled on either side of her (baby brother Paulie must have been off-camera in his crib). Mom is peering down through her black-framed harlequin glasses at the guitar chord she's fingering, a chord that her other beautiful hand, with its "artistic" long fingers, has just strummed.

For me this picture is very symbolic because it shows my mother at the center of things but looking distracted, as though unaware that everyone is gathered around her. You could say that my mother was the star of our family but not through any focused effort on her part; she was the star simply through the absentminded force of her personality, her moods. She was the preoccupied sun around which we all—dogs, cats, children, husband—orbited. She was the kind of mom who'd stay in the car while we kids romped around on the beach with Dad on a windy, exhilarating April afternoon. When we climbed back into the car we'd find the engine running and Mom deep in an atmosphere of loud baroque music on the radio. "I was watching you all to this beautiful music," she'd say. "Isn't life weird?" That was Mom. Though she hadn't participated in things, she and her comment became what I remembered of that day.

My mother's moods filled our house like a strong, mysterious perfume. She was always picking at her face at the kitchen window where she'd balanced a small round mirror on the sill. From time to time we kids would come up to tell her things, and though she often seemed to be in her own world, her mind obviously far away, she'd murmur very generous, approving little nothings when we fell silent. "That's great, honey, you're really something. I'm so proud of you." For me the faraway quality of her moods was most present in the folk music she continually played on our old-fashioned stereo that was quite an impressive piece of furniture—a huge mahogany thing with two large speakers covered with fabric that seemed to me spun of the brightest gold threads. Sometimes I'd sit with my ear practically pressed to one of these large gold speakers. Pouring out from it would be Joan Baez's martyred, fine-china voice singing Bob Dylan's "Sad Eyed Lady of the Lowlands," a song so long and enchanted that it took up one entire scratchy side of an LP.

My mother's music was the ruling spirit of our house. My sister Susie and I liked to tease her about her habit of running a favorite song into the ground, playing it twenty times in a row. But as the 1960s wore on the records Mom played were no laughing matter to her, reflecting the overall darkening of her mood—her despair, really—though we kids had no idea of its depths. Today my mother says she still can't bear to hear the Bee Gees song "I Started a Joke" because it brings back all the feelings that went into her suicide attempts and hospitalizations that began to take place in the late sixties. As a kid for whom much of my mother was elusive (I never knew at the time, for instance, just why she was in the hospital), I could never have imagined that one of the lines in this Bee Gees song—"When

I finally died, it started the whole world living"—was something Mom took to heart because she'd become convinced that Dad and we kids would all be much better off with her dead.

The odd thing is that I, who ended up taking after my mother's side, the White side, of the family, saw things quite differently as a child. As a little kid it was the Fleming side I felt at home with and the Whites who were alien. The worlds of my divorced maternal grandparents, Delilah and E. V. White, otherwise such different planets, were alike in having no real place for children. As a baby I'd called Delilah "Nanny" (rhymes with Bonny) and the name had stuck. Nanny's high-rise apartment on the fifty-eighth floor of Marina Towers in downtown Chicago was filled with fragile, precious, spotless things that we were always being warned not to touch. When you opened Nanny's little refrigerator you never found much in there—just some soda water, a lemon or two, and a bottle of maraschino cherries that we weren't allowed to open. Going to see her was as dull and formal as visiting a museum. Yes, the view from the fifty-eighth floor was spectacular, but the charm of it wore off soon enough and the hours would drag on as the grown-ups dawdled over the meal Nanny had served out on her tiny cement slab of a balcony up in the clouds, a setting made still more uncomfortable for us kids by the wrought-iron chairs you had to sit in out there. Everything about Nanny's luxury apartment struck me and my little brother and sister as terribly cramped and uninviting. The few things that excited our imagination about Marina Towers were forbidden us: holding elevator races, or lingering down in the garage where the black car attendants parked visiting autos by racing them around and around the upward-spiraling ramps, returning back to earth carless via a fascinating little elevator of their own that was little more than a motorized moving ladder that they clung to with nonchalant grace in their grimy coveralls. In the summer of 1968 when I was nine I happened to spend a couple weeks at Grandpa White's in Cincinnati followed by still more weeks at Grandma and Grandpa Fleming's in Cleveland. I can't remember why exactly I'd been shipped off like this. Perhaps this was when Mom was in the hospital and my father needed a break. Or maybe this was one of the times Mom and Dad were trying to patch things up by taking a canoe trip together up in Canada. In any event, within Grandpa White's large, hushed house, which was even less child-friendly than Nanny's high-rise, I could not have felt any less at home had I been set down in a medieval palace flickering in torchlight. My mother was always telling me what a great baseball player Grandpa White had been as a young man but he and I never played catch, never did anything together. I don't know that I even saw Grandpa during that visit. He had his nocturnal schedule to keep to, after all, working alone throughout the night at his company, White Industrial Sales & Equipment Co., because my mother said he disliked people and wanted to avoid seeing his own employees.

It's Grandpa's wife Kay, the wicked stepmother of Mom's girlhood, that comes to mind. I remember standing with Kay in her enormous, well-stocked kitchen, and her asking me point-blank, "How many times a week do you eat steak at your house?" Somehow I picked up on the snobby drift of the question enough to know that I should lie: I told her that we had steak two or three times a week, when in fact my father's modest salary meant that Mom served up mostly meatloaf, hamburgers, and fish sticks. Early on Kay had also taken me on what she called, in her drawling, braying voice, "the grand tour." In fact, there was not much to see of the house. The many closed doors upstairs were not to be opened, she said, because behind most of them lay cats, who because of fighting had each been placed in the regal isolation of its own room. No, the grand tour consisted mostly of examining the dozens of oil paintings Kay herself had painted and mounted everywhere, including halfway down the basement stairs, each beachscape or portrait of Rasputin lit up like a masterpiece under its own little gooseneck spotlight. I don't think I'd learned yet to make phony compliments—I was just a kid who shifted from foot to foot in this kind of weird situation.

Anyway, for the rest of the visit I was on my own for hours at a time in a house where I was afraid to turn on the TV or even occupy space. I found myself spending most of my time outdoors, pretending I was in the Olympics (it was an Olympic summer) by running through the surrounding suburban lanes that were themselves weirdly childless and deserted looking. What a relief to arrive at the Fleming Fowl Farm, as Grandma and Grandpa Fleming still called their acre or so of land though it had now been a couple years since they'd shut down the chicken farm. Grandpa Fleming had sold off much of his land so that an elementary school could be built, a school where he himself now served as the janitor. The chicken coop, still white-splotched inside and reeking of chicken shit, now housed the studio of my father's youngest brother, my Uncle Bill, who attended a local art college. Unlike my grandfather's wife Kay, Uncle Bill was not stuck up about art or anything else. I slept in his room in the upper berth of his bunkbed and before turning in we'd listen to the Beatles together on his record player/radio, a freestanding thing that stood as tall as a wooden refrigerator and whose dial glowed a beautiful yellow in the dark. Uncle Bill, handsome with his long dark brown hair and mustache, looked a bit like a Beatle himself.

There was always plenty of fun stuff to do around the Fowl Farm. The childhoods of my father and his other brothers had left behind big canvas bags full of bats, balls, and batting helmets, and there was even a baseball diamond out beyond the old chicken coop. Here Uncle Bill would whack fly balls high into the air that I would shag in the outfield grass that Grandpa Fleming kept so beautifully mowed with his tractor. Grandpa Fleming hardly ever said anything but there wasn't any mystery to him. He was a natural silent type and particularly now that his hearing was going and he felt too embarrassed to wear hearing aids, he'd become a completely nonverbal presence who just

sat in a lawn chair under a shade tree drinking green bottles of
Rolling Rock beer, his face itself green from the light shining
through the green visor on his cap. In his silent, somewhat
rough way he was very sweet to me. According to my mother,
his people had been Kentucky hillbillies and Grandpa had left
school after only the eighth grade. Grandpa would sometimes
fire up his noisy tractor and let me take the wheel as we shud-
dered along at two miles per hour down the graveled horseshoe
driveway. Or he'd surprise me as I passed by him in his easy
chair, where he'd be sitting watching a baseball game on television, capturing me in the vise of his strong legs—a game that
he called "bear trap." I'd feel like a nut in a nutcracker, and after
struggling furiously for a minute would be tempted to cry out
for help, but Grandpa always released the bear trap just when I
was getting really flushed and panicky. For him, of course, the
whole thing was a big show of affection.

At Grandpa White's house things had been so strained that
for all the food on hand, in pantry cupboards and their super-
duper refrigerator, I'd gone to bed a little hungry each night.
Grandma Fleming, however, had raised several sons and knew
just what little boys like me liked to eat. There were always
plenty of peanut butter sandwiches and tall glasses of milk into
which she mixed a few teaspoons of powdered Strawberry Quik.
Even better, there were three male cousins roughly my age, the
sons of my father's oldest brother, who lived nearby and were
always ready to play.

In sharp contrast, my mother's only sibling, my Uncle Eddie,
had no children. He lived in a city that itself seemed to have no
children, for all its vast crowds and noise. I don't think I ever
got to see the Upper West Side apartment that Uncle Eddie
shared with his friend Stanley, which was too small for us relatives to stay in when we came to town. Mom would laugh about
this apartment, saying it was "a real wreck," with a dining room
table that had no legs and was supported instead on top of boxes.
And so when we visited Uncle Eddie in New York in the sixties
we would put ourselves up at an old midtown hotel that might

as well have been in Russia for all the old carpets and smells in
the halls, the creaking elevator, the gray bedsheets in the
cramped, shabby rooms. All of New York City seemed gray with
history and overuse, and shockingly run-down—an annoying
place where there was nowhere to play.

My mother and Uncle Eddie had been introduced to a quite
different Manhattan when they were kids: the Manhattan that
money can buy. Their father, E.V., would make periodic business trips to the city, which in those days before jet travel were
made via Cadillac—a long drive that would begin with nocturnal
E.V. nosing out of his Cincinnati garage at midnight, his dozing
family waking up only when dawn was breaking over the mountains of Pennsylvania. By the dinner hour they'd be pulling up
in front of E.V.'s favorite midtown hotel, the Roosevelt, ready
to freshen up and head out for an evening at Asti's, a restaurant
so musical that even the waiters would take turns singing arias.
My own childhood trips to the city, however, involved spending
the day atop the Empire State Building before meeting up with
Uncle Eddie at a Chinese restaurant, something that struck me
as appropriate, since my mother had said Eddie majored in Chinese of all things at college. In his own benevolent way Uncle
Eddie could be just as at sea around children as were Grandpa
White, Kay, and Nanny. My mother loved to tell the story of
the time Eddie was given an infant to hold and had acted as
though he were handling something alien and very fragile, a
radioactive moonrock that had to be held out from his body.
"How do you do?" was the only thing he could think to say
to it.

Uncle Eddie could definitely be a little weird. As a third
grader, I was accustomed to adults giving me only the briefest,
impersonal approval whenever I'd scribbled some little piece of
writing. How startling therefore to hear what Uncle Eddie had
to say when Mom suddenly put me on the phone with him. My
mother had filled him in on my latest "story" (really just a par-
agraph, I think) about Count Dracula waking up in his coffin to
a slowly opening, creaking lid. Now I was holding the phone to

my ear and listening as Uncle Eddie advised me to do a complete rewrite: "Hitchcock's films, you know, have shown us that what's *really* scary emerges from what *seems* to be normal, everyday life. And so instead of Dracula's castle, I think maybe something like your own home out there in Evanston might be a better setting for the horrors to come." I was neither prepared nor pleased to be taken so seriously. Part of me was intrigued but mostly I was just overwhelmed by such drastic, sophisticated advice. I had no idea that it was not unprecedented for boys my age to write— that Uncle Eddie, for instance, had written a whole play in three acts, *The Blue Bird*, when he was a third grader.

No, Uncle Eddie was still a very small presence in my life, someone I'd forget about for months and months at a time as I went about playing the sports that my mother said Eddie had been so horrible at as a boy that he'd never been invited to join a single baseball, basketball, or football team. Still, by fifth grade the door in my mind had opened a bit wider to Uncle Eddie's opinions. My mother let me read a letter Eddie had sent her after our most recent visit to New York, a letter in which he mentioned in passing that I had struck him as being "very sincere and reflective." It was the first time I'd heard myself described. As I read the words they seemed invested with such authority that I felt just as though I'd been X-rayed and here was the result.

As the sixties wore on my mother too was taking Eddie more and more seriously. She'd stopped seeing her little brother as being an embarrassment one rainy night in 1963 when she happened to witness dozens of people lining up in the rain to see Eddie's play *The Blue Boy in Black*, which was being produced off-Broadway with the young Billy Dee Williams and Cicely Tyson as costars. Eddie also looked so much better now that he'd moved to New York. As a boy he'd been very nerdy-looking with his close-cropped hair, glasses, and big ears sticking out from his large head. But now in New York he'd gotten contact lenses, wore his hair longer, and had filled out with age so that his ears rode closer to his skull. By the mid-sixties, when I first

started hearing about him, Eddie had become a colorful, diverting character in my mother's mind—someone who'd moved
to New York by flying first-class despite having no job lined up
there and only a few hundred dollars to his name. And so the
only Eddie that I myself had ever known was a handsome, almost
Italian-looking uncle with a dark mane of expensively cut hair,
brown eyes that looked at you with merry compassion, and a
knack for making my mother act much more alive whenever he
was around.

By 1971, the year that she divorced Dad, Mom had come to see
Eddie as her hero. That was also the year that Uncle Eddie
started truly coming into focus for me over the course of a long
Thanksgiving weekend that my mother, brother, sister, and I all
spent with him. Uncle Eddie picked us up at JFK in a borrowed
station wagon and drove us far out on Long Island to a house
he'd rented for the weekend. Mom giggled as Eddie explained
that he'd never roasted a turkey before and had been shocked
that morning to find it frozen solid in the icebox. The bird was
now thawing out in a hot bath he'd drawn for it. Waiting for
us at the house along with the submerged turkey were two
women friends of Eddie's—his longtime friend Marilyn Schaefer, whom I knew, and a strange younger woman Eddie took to
calling "Crazy Judy" when she was out of earshot. Crazy Judy,
very pretty with her masses of wild brown hair, was the first
person I'd met who would suddenly just take off, running away
without word or warning or even a reason that I could see. We
were walking the cold November shore of Long Island Sound
the next afternoon—Uncle Eddie, my little brother, Crazy Judy,
and I—when Crazy Judy took off, kicking up sand and spray as
she galloped far, far down the beach away from us. Still more
strangely, she really took her time coming back to us, moving
very slowly with her hands held behind her back, looking mood-
ily out to sea, at shells by her feet, anywhere but at us, though
we were all staring at her. Maybe this was when Uncle Eddie
dubbed her "Crazy Judy."

At twelve I wasn't yet in the habit of speculating about people's motives or about the interpersonal weather between adults. I still tended to see things with a child's simple fatalism. My parents' recent divorce, for instance, had struck me as a kind of terrible car accident that had befallen us out of the blue. Only by dent of my mother's new and constant mockery of my father behind his back was it slowly dawning on me that such a thing existed as complex incompatibility between people. And so I didn't give any thought to what might be up between Crazy Judy and Uncle Eddie. After she'd rejoined us I got caught up with my little brother in playing a game I'd invented where we crept right up to the water's edge and then darted away at the last possible instant from the incoming ocean surf. The surging, foaming power of the ocean awed and delighted me because I was a midwestern boy familiar with only the tiny waves of Lake Michigan—kids' stuff, I realized now.

Back at our rented house I happily ignored Uncle Eddie and the women as they tended to our Thanksgiving dinner (the turkey had successfully thawed out in its hot bath and was now roasting away in the oven). My brother and I glued ourselves to the TV and the big college football game being played between Nebraska and Oklahoma. This monumental showdown was something the sports pages had been trumpeting for weeks as irresistible force (Oklahoma) meets immovable object (Nebraska), but I knew enough about my uncle by now to know that he cared as little for such things as my mother did. The next morning over breakfast, though, Uncle Eddie really got my attention. He told us that Crazy Judy, still upstairs sleeping, had come to him in the middle of the night in her nightgown and climbed into bed with him, whimpering about how she'd had a nightmare and needed comforting. Crazy Judy, I realized, was completely crazy about Uncle Eddie.

Later that day I found myself wondering idly whether Crazy Judy had supplanted Marilyn Schaefer as the woman Eddie was considering marrying. I'd often heard my mother and grandmother remark that "Eddie doesn't do well living by himself" and that he and Marilyn sometimes talked about getting married. But when I took Mom aside to ask if she knew which woman Eddie preferred, my mother assumed such a heavy, unnatural air that I knew even before she said anything that something funny was up.

Speaking in a strangely careful voice that seemed not so much directed at me as at something only her upraised, abstracted eyes could see, she told me, "Well, actually, honey, neither. You see . . . well, Uncle Eddie is—well, honey, he's gay. Do you have any idea what that means?"

I said that I did, but in fact I didn't. Not really. On the playground I'd heard about boys who were little perverts and played around with each other, but I couldn't apply this to Uncle Eddie. No, Uncle Eddie was "gay," which seemed like something utterly different, something as sophisticated as everything else about him. Maybe a better way to put it is that I wasn't in the habit of imagining what anyone else, particularly family members, did in the bedroom with clothes off. For me Uncle Eddie was, like all the adults in my life, entirely what he appeared to be in the living room. And so to hear that he was gay was like finally having a name for the personal style, always so exotic and theatrical, that Uncle Eddie had been putting on display throughout my childhood. The way he lit up the room, for instance, as unendingly as he lit up his Kent cigarettes (my mother occasionally bought a pack of Virginia Slims but it was a shock to accompany Uncle Eddie to the local drugstore and watch him purchase not a pack but *two cartons* of Kents). I can still see him sitting on our modest living room couch, one leg draped femininely over his knee in the fashionably tattered jeans he'd bought "pre-ripped" from a MacDougal Street shop. He's telling a story that's making my mother bark with laughter (about a "nutty man" who announced to Eddie at a party that he spoke eight languages but then added that "Henglish" was his best). But what most holds my attention is the easy, almost musical rising and falling of his voice, the way the silvery-quick flow of words sometimes slows to a kind of purring emphasis at key points in the story—and all this while elegant jets of smoke are regularly coming out his nostrils!

Since sexual identity plays such a big role in my family, the story of my own boyish sexuality has a place here. For, as it happened, the next time I saw my uncle after learning he was gay I could hardly wait for his stories and the evening to end. We'd all gathered for a Christmas weekend at my grandmother Delilah's "country place," as she called the ordinary suburban house on the Michigan shore that she used on weekends. I was impatient for everyone to call it a night because I'd been assigned the living room sofa for my bed and I was itching to be alone under the covers where I could resume the thrilling voyage into pleasure I'd just discovered: jerking off. The miracle of masturbation was so powerful, so intensely personal, that it almost seemed like my own invention. Certainly I would have found it hard to believe that my talky adult family members, Uncle Eddie included, knew anything even approaching the feverish ecstasy I was now indulging in nearly every night.

Maybe the reason that other people's sex lives didn't seem quite real to me was just that I was so caught up in my own. Even so my first orgasm, achieved just a few months earlier, had come as a nasty, unwelcome surprise. Far from relishing the experience, I'd recoiled in horror from this convulsion I'd unintentionally provoked. Nothing I'd learned in fifth grade Sex Ed class had prepared me for the violent reality of coming because Mr. Henderson, our teacher, had spoken only of the dull microscopic doings of sperm and egg. He made sex seem an impersonal business and nothing he'd said so much as hinted that if a boy persisted in playing with his boner it would start spasming and spurting out milky fluid like jets of blood pumping from a severed artery. That's what had been so scary—the wild moment when I thought I'd badly hurt myself somehow. What a relief when the convulsion stopped and I turned out to be okay after all.

It took weeks to get used to orgasm and see it as the goal of

my labors and not a penalty. For when I'd first started playing
with myself I'd hit upon, in my innocence, a technique almost
Oriental in its sustained balancing upon the brink of ejaculation.
I'd gotten hold of one of my father's old neckties and started
stroking the entire tingling shaft of my boner with a silky width
of necktie held taut in my hands. By steadily thrumming myself
in this way I was soon inducing brighter thrills of pleasure than
I've been able to find since. Funny how a kid unwittingly tan-
talizing his poor hard-on can leap to the very peak of animal
sexuality, to the body's capacity for ecstasy.

But by focusing on whacking off I'm leaving out the roman-
ticism about girls that fueled everything. My sessions with the
necktie would go on so long that whole stories had time to form
and play themselves out in my imagination while I thrummed
away. For instance: I happen to be walking along the shoulder
of a highway—not going anywhere, just walking along—and
come across a girl hitchhiker. Fortunately we're in the middle
of nowhere and there are no cars going by. She looks like a very
young Linda Ronstadt, though she's a bit older than I am—
fourteen, say. We walk off the road into the fields and seat ourselves in the high grass. We're deep in conversation. We're best
friends. She takes off her clothes. She and I have infinite time
for each other, and infinite interest, and this is what had been
missing from life. We don't need anything or anyone and are
just going to keep traveling around together, having these talks
and this sex and riding this high.

Romantic thoughts had actually been welling up in me since
the first grade. One night back then I'd sniffed the water glass
on my night table and found it mysteriously smelling of a kind
of heavenly cherry cola. And leaping out of this delightful smell,
so it seemed to me, was the very essence of my first grade
teacher, glamorous Miss De Haun, whose silver-blonde hair
would tickle my neck with its loose strands whenever she leaned
over my desk to hand back some papers. By third grade my
romantic imagination had taken on a mild naughtiness. I now
had a crush on a classmate, Lisa, that I would keep faithfully to

myself all through third and fourth grades. From our classroom windows a stand of woods was visible at the back of the school grounds, and in my daydreams Lisa sat naked with me in this little wilderness. I don't think I was naked myself. The chief excitement seemed to be the privilege of being permitted to view *her* nakedness.

And then one day a boy classmate confided to me the dirty secret of fucking. It was all a bit vague but very exciting, particularly the highly charged word *fuck* itself. My friend had acquired his information from an older brother—the rumor being that big boys sometimes stuck their dick into a girl's. Oddly, my friend used the word *dick* to refer to both male and female genitals. He even had a joke involving a character named Inspector Dick whose name became a play on words: *inspect her dick*. A year or so later another classmate's more experienced older brother gave me a better peek into the world of sex. I was over at their house one day and this brother, a high school student, led us up to the bedroom he'd recently fashioned for himself at the top of the house. It was impressively hard just to get to it. First, you entered a walk-in closet. There, in the dark, you found and climbed up a ladder. When we'd all made it to the top, the brother dropped in a wood panel that sealed the trapdoor behind us. He'd created a zone, I realized, that was inaccessible to prying parents. But we still hadn't reached his room. Now we had to put one foot before the other as we balanced ourselves along wooden beams that crisscrossed the length of the attic above sunken parts of the floor covered in pink insulation.

Finally we reached his room, a self-contained lair he'd set up on the far side of the attic by means of tall screens whose infacing sides he'd lined with tinfoil. When he put *Sgt. Pepper* on the record player and got out his store of *Playboy* magazines, I'd thought the atmosphere was more than complete. But no. The final touch was the tales he told us of bringing girls up here. The latest one had been here just yesterday. She'd gotten comfortable right away, letting him put his hands under her bra and then take her whole top off. Next: her underpants. It was hot down there and not every girl would let you slip your fingers under the elastic band to touch her there. . . .

But I don't remember hearing him brag about actually fucking a girl. What stays with me is how real his girl seemed, how the tinfoil in his hideaway seemed to shimmer with her presence and the possibilities she offered.

It surprised me to hear how cooperative and even openly willing the girls he knew acted because all my fantasies were built upon the premise that girls were reluctant to go along with boys' funny stuff. During the many idle hours I spent lying in the back of our station wagon on family trips, I'd dreamt up a crazy TV game show where the number of points accumulated by the contestant (me) was then directly translated into an even cruder reward than money. For racking up a hundred points meant winning the right to insert my penis into a girl for a hundred minutes. Because I didn't know yet about orgasm and the mechanics of intercourse, insertion was something I imagined as a very static thing. You stuck it in her and then the two of you just sat there together for a hundred wonderful minutes. That seemed quite thrilling enough. After all, the very word *vagina* had a sexy magic to it that never wore off no matter how many times I looked it up in the dictionary, always a little astounded that it was even listed in there.

Soon I was acting out in real life my notion that games were needed to coax a girl into sex play. Kimberly, a girl who lived down the street, a friend of my sister's, was someone whose prettiness and frequent presence around our house inspired me to invent "Seeing the King," a game where I was a king that everyone had to come see privately in the attic. Our second floor had been all attic when my parents first bought the house but my father had converted it into a giant bedroom/playroom for me and my little brother, installing floor tiles and windows and painting the walls a cheerful green. Only a corner of the old attic was left intact, walled off from the rest of the floor. It was in this dark dusty chamber, where cobwebs hung from the low sloping ceiling to the rough wood floorboards, that I would meet with my royal subjects. Because the little attic lacked electric outlets, I had to bring in a candle to light the place: the whole purpose of the game would be defeated if I couldn't see. Because though decency required that I receive absolutely everybody and suffer through dull interviews one at a time with my sister and brother and any friends of my brother's who happened to be around, the secret point to it all was when Kimberly walked in and I had her to myself for a few minutes. It had been established between us that she would walk back and forth before me in the nude at some point during every interview. It might even have been her idea to parade around like this. I as the king had probably only requested that she strip off her clothes. Anyway, I remember it was definitely her own idea to practice doing "the splits" in front of me occasionally.

Kimberly had a belly button that was a slight "outie" but otherwise her body struck me as perfection. Interestingly, once she'd slipped out of her last piece of clothing, her pink underpants, and I'd adjusted myself to her nudity, it was not just the pudgy skin of her labia or her smooth little rear end that caught my admiring eye but her whole beautiful honey-colored ten-year-old-girl body—her slim, fresh arms and legs tapering to delicate wrists and ankles, her flat, pink-nippled chest, the way her body was lean enough to show her rib cage clearly yet had everywhere a soft pad of feminine baby fat. Somehow I had already become a connoisseur of female bodies, with quite definite ideas about which girls I wanted to see naked. Word about what Kimberly and I were up to in the attic eventually got out to two other little girls on the block, who let it be known that they too were willing to strip for the king, but I never took them up on it. Only Kimberly's body excited me.

At some point I started pulling down my own pants while she paraded to and fro, though it was Kimberly who was the natural exhibitionist. My mother told me that Kimberly's mom had let Kimberly run around without any clothes on for the first five years of her life, a practice that resulted in Kimberly's being sent home from her first day of kindergarten when she stripped off

her unaccustomed clothes in the middle of quiet time. Now at
ten Kimberly often said she wanted to be a Playboy bunny when
she grew up. She was so much more comfortable with nudity
than I was that though I never once touched her, she did touch
me a couple times—if *touch* is the word. For as I would stand
there with my pants pushed down to my knees, Kimberly would
flounce past me and my erection and occasionally bat at it with
the back of her hand the way you'd flick away a balloon a ma--
gician had twisted into a comical shape.

There was no denying that exposing myself constituted a
whole new thrill; it also made me feel more a part of the game.
But just as I was getting into the swing of things, puberty came
out of nowhere to bring an end to my days with Kimberly as
king of the attic. Pubic hair was the culprit. I found this un-
wanted hair growing in to be so hateful that I took one of my
mother's disposable razors and shaved it all right off. It wasn't
that I was reluctant to grow up or anything (like most kids, I
spent a lot of time wishing I were years older). No, the problem
with pubic hair was simply that it put a serious damper on my
sex life—on my sex play with Kimberly. I saw it as a cosmetic
disaster, something as embarrassing and conspicuous as a big
pimple on the ass, something that would only provoke laughter
and questions. Displaying a boner was already awkward enough,
I felt, without having to display one with hair all around it. No,
that was asking too much—I just couldn't do it. And once I
discovered how incredibly itchy it was to have shaved hair growing back in down there, I gave up trying to reverse things and
put myself under wraps for good.

Everywhere I looked that spring of 1971 my childhood was ending. My mother and father had finally gone through with their
divorce after three years of separations, and now that I'd turned
twelve I was playing my final Little League baseball season. One
of the many ramifications of the new divorce was that Mom and
Dad had to take turns attending my games in order to avoid
seeing each other. Twice that spring when it was my mother's

turn to sit in the stands and cheer me on, she brought her father, my Grandpa White, along with her. Grandpa had been living in the Chicago area for the past two years but it was only following my parents' divorce that we started to see much of him. He'd bought a house in Lake Forest, a spacious suburb of mansions a dozen miles up the lake shore from us in Evanston, and for several months Grandpa had been all on his own in his big new house, since his wife Kay refused to leave Cincinnati and her lady friends from the Keyboard Club, which she considered the pinnacle of high society there. But Kay had finally steeled herself to the idea of exile and joined Grandpa in Lake Forest, bringing with her her microwave oven and her many difficult cats.

With Grandpa White suddenly around, and my father suddenly absent, it was impossible not to think of Grandpa as a kind of replacement for Dad, since Grandpa was now the man at my mother's side in the car and in the Little League bleachers. Strangely enough, two of the three home runs I ever hit were struck with Grandpa looking on. Strange, because I'd always found Grandpa White—so big and commanding—extremely intimidating to be around. He was definitely the eight-hundred-pound gorilla of the family. When my mother was on the phone with him and called out to me, "Honey, Grandpa wants to say hi to you," I'd approach the phone very slowly, like a doomed man, because I never knew what to say to him (it never occurred to me Grandpa preferred it that I stay quiet because he was happiest when doing all the talking). But somehow I'd managed to do my best hitting with him on hand and my mother said that each time I'd hit a home run Grandpa stood up and bellowed for all to hear, "That's my grandson, goddamnit!" She said Grandpa was "just bursting with pride" because he'd always wanted a son to follow in his footsteps as a ballplayer (Uncle Eddie's playing, apparently, was remembered only for the time he got hit in the head with a fly ball). But though my mother claimed Grandpa was so proud of me that he'd given me his ultimate seal of approval, saying of me, "You know, I think I like him," I could never quite believe it.

No, for me Grandpa White was always more a stranger than a grandfather, someone who would hold us captive in his cold, smoky Cadillac. With the windows sealed, the air-conditioning on full blast even at night, and his cigar smoke slowly poisoning us, the interior of his Cadillac was very much a hostile climate— like being locked in a polluted meat freezer, really. And as if that wasn't enough there was his relentless talking about the proper cultivation of the tobacco plant. And the fact that Italians should not be considered a part of the white race. And the necessity of paying for everything, including cars and houses, in cash. And the outrage of this new rapid transit line running down the center of the Kennedy Expressway that allowed unemployed black riders to sit there in train cars that whizzed right up alongside our Cadillac—that even started pulling ahead of us, goddamnit!

Grandpa certainly seemed to see life as one big competition. Watching me hit home runs must have gotten his competitive juices flowing, I guess, because back at home he surprised me by challenging me to a bicycle race. It seemed like a very weird idea because Grandpa was now an old-looking sixty-six with liver spots, a heart condition, and a very unathletic wardrobe consisting of business suits and wing-tip shoes. As we mounted our bikes in the middle of the street and got set to race the one-block sprint he'd laid out, I wondered just how humiliating this was going to be for him. I politely got off to a lazy start but when he shot out into the lead, I started racing for real and overtook him. What happened next is my defining memory of Grandpa White. Surging back into the corner of my vision, he— incredibly—drew himself even with me. He'd risen off his seat by now and was leaning far out over the handlebars, like a jockey on a horse, and though my mother claims to have heard him bellowing "Hi ho, Texas!" I just remember the sight of his legs furiously pumping in his gray flannel pants that were flapping high up around his bone-white shins. Neck and neck we roared down the stretch but in the last ten yards Grandpa somehow came up with a final burst that let him streak to victory. I was stunned—frightened, really. His face toward the end had been almost demonic in its flushed, maniacal grimacing. I'd never witnessed such straining, vein-popping effort up close like that. I'd never seen anyone want something so badly.

It had been a crazy expense of energy and a day or two later Grandpa suffered a serious heart attack. He spent weeks recovering in the hospital and my mother said it was a good thing he didn't die right there on the bike. Upon his discharge, he and Kay decided to move back to Cincinnati—"Cincinaduh," as they called it—where Grandpa could recuperate in semiretirement and Kay rejoin her Keyboard Club. Though Grandpa White survived several more years, he was never an active part of our lives again. Whenever we'd ask them for money, Kay would always say they'd sure love to help out but things were a little tight right now.

Right after Grandpa White left town a big change came over our house: Mom's new friend Ricki and her three kids moved in with us. My mother had gotten to know Ricki, a very suburban-looking housewife with light brown hair cut in a pageboy, at a weekly therapy group she attended down in the city. Ricki was in the midst of the same kind of deep dissatisfaction with her life and marriage that my mother had just gone through. Mom told me that Ricki's husband, a Korean-born biochemist, had had the toes on one foot blown off when he stepped on a land mine as a young soldier. Apparently Dr. Kim's stump foot was always leaving scratches on Ricki in bed. But recently when Ricki asked him to move out, Dr. Kim not only refused but took to running around the house turning off all the lights because he didn't see why he should pay the electric bills if Ricki wasn't happy being his wife. And so when Ricki told Mom one night after group that she couldn't stand it anymore, that being in the same house with him was making her physically ill, Mom invited Ricki and her kids to come and take refuge at our place.

Suddenly my mother was happy again. The records she played

on the stereo had always been the register of her moods and
now the song playing over and over again was Cat Stevens'
"Morning Has Broken." Though glad to see our mother feeling
so chipper, my sister and I quickly got so sick of "Morning Has
Broken" that we started telling her we wished the record was
broken. Ricki, however, seemed as enchanted by the song as our
mother was and sometimes even sang it a cappella at Mom's
request. Ricki had a trained voice (she'd once dreamed of being
an opera singer) and it was striking to hear her so fluent in song
because as a speaker she suffered from terrible fits of stuttering.
In a cruel stroke of fate, words beginning with *r* constituted her
biggest stumbling block and thus her own name gave her some
of her worst trouble. Ricki's stuttering was unlike anything I'd
ever heard. It wasn't a constant, low-level accompaniment to her
speech that you could get used to, but rather an occasional, spectacular snagging—like a car unable to get going on a patch of
ice no matter how much the engine is gunned. Particularly on
the phone this hopeless gunning of her engine could be so
wrenching and prolonged that when it was Ricki on the line
("Hi, this is Ruh-Ruh-Ruh-Ruh-Ruh—"), my brother, sister,
and I felt free to interject, "Oh hi, Ricki, let me get my mom,"
and lay down the phone with her still "Ruh"-ing away.

But we kids became very fond of Ricki, and she of us. Thanks
to her we were now eating much better. Our mother had never
been very interested in cooking and we'd grown up on the hap-
hazard meals she threw together at the last minute: frozen peas
or corn kernels, burned meat loaf, and iceberg lettuce smothered
in Thousand Island dressing. How delicious and new to sit down
to carefully planned and prepared dinners (Ricki used the oven!):
pork and pot roasts, hams, baked potatoes slathered in sour
cream with chives, apple pies made from scratch. Still, my
mother's cooking had had its memorable moments. Who could
forget her dangerous morning "hambies"—as she called the
breakfast hamburgers she said she needed to eat because without
their protein she'd get the shakes? These breakfast hambies were
fried each morning in a skillet still greasy from the previous

morning's hambie so that a sudden burst of flame would always shoot up five feet into the air at some point—a phenomenon that only made my mother laugh as she expertly dodged out of the way.

Ricki was also different from Mom in being an immaculate housekeeper. She slept on a perfect little bed she constructed each night on the plaid couch in the living room out of freshly laundered pillowcases and neatly tucked-in sheets and blankets. Ricki even took it upon herself to redo our living room, painting it a mustard yellow with crisp white trim and hanging up some sheer white curtains she'd bought at Sears. My mother was thrilled by the home improvement because during the last few turbulent years of marriage to Dad the house had been slowly falling into disrepair. Still, there were limits to what even Ricki was willing to take on, and after getting an eyeful of the state of the upstairs, where two of her kids were now sleeping with me and my brother, Ricki decided just to let things go up there, where heaps of cast-off clothes were already accumulating.

I never felt put out much by the newly crowded state of affairs at our house. When Ricki and her kids moved in, I decided to construct a lair for myself in what remained of the old attic. By dragging my mattress and box spring in there, along with an extension cord, I found I could tame this shadowy, spidery place to my satisfaction by fitting it out with a lamp and a radio. True, the attic would always be dusty, airless, and hot; and there was no denying it was a cramped, windowless corner of the house where one needed to stoop as one moved around under the low, sloping ceiling of the roof overhead. But who cared about that when you could finally have a place all to yourself for a change? I'd shared the fixed-up part of the upstairs for years with my little brother, and though it was fun sometimes to play tackle football all over our shared bedroom, or wake each other up with farts whose various timbres we gave names to, it did seem like high time I had some privacy (a privacy I could make absolute by using the hook I'd installed on the inner side of the door). Then too, the attic air still tingled for me with the

naughty secret magic of all the times I'd ogled Kimberly's nakedness by candlelight.

Ricki's three children, two girls and a boy, all possessed beautiful Eurasian features (their father, Dr. Kim, must have been
extremely handsome because Ricki's kids were all much prettier
than she was). I was immediately drawn to the eldest child,
eleven-year-old Stephanie. Because Stephanie was about my sister's age, it was decided that she should share my sister's
downstairs bedroom with her, while the two younger Kim kids
made a big mess upstairs with my little brother. Soon, however,
Stephanie was spending much of her time upstairs with me in
the attic. For young as she was, Stephanie was already a confident flirt who in no time at all had initiated me into "the ways,"
by which she meant the many different ways we could curl up
and hold each other on my mattress. Somehow my mother, who
never ventured upstairs anymore, sensed right away that something was going on between me and Stephanie—how did she
know, I wondered: witchcraft?—embarrassing me by warning
me I'd better not be "doing it" with her.

My mother needn't have worried. It was all very puppy love
and Stephanie and I never so much as took off any of our
clothes. No, I found it quite thrilling enough to wrap my arms
around Stephanie's warm, cooperative body, stroke her long curtain of fine, silky hair, and know this powerful new intimacy with
someone. Stephanie would lay her head on my chest this way
and that, the two of us speaking in a tender whisper I'd never
used before, and her silky hair would brush my face as she
climbed over to the other side of me where we tried out yet
another way, this one with her back to me and my interlocking
hands around her soft belly, whose heat I could feel through her
T-shirt. Her hair smelled wonderfully of fruity shampoo. I
would have found it impossible to ask her to do anything like
strip for me because this intimacy of ours, the whole tenor of
our tenderness, made stuff like the king game seem vulgar. Of
course, much of the carefree lechery I'd felt around Kimberly
had been due to Kimberly's own exhibitionism, but it also sprang

on my side from a complete emotional detachment. I hadn't felt anything for Kimberly but lust to see her naked. Now with Stephanie I felt almost too much. I felt romantic, and with romance came reverence and shyness. I was like a new vinyl record, and my passion was very clear and bright in me as the needle made its first pass through my feelings for her.

But soon I was crazy to see her naked. She spent a lot of time in our one bathroom, washing her hair more than once a day, and my desire to see the thrilling nudity existing just beyond the locked bathroom door reached such a fever pitch that I hit upon a simple, daring scheme. Between our house and the next ran a narrow passageway all overgrown with wild bushes and weeds that was known mainly to the neighborhood cats. It was in this passageway that one evening under cover of darkness I stood a ladder up against the house just below the bathroom window. Because the window's three lower panes had been painted over, my next step was to scrape clear, as inconspicuous as I could make it, the tiniest slit that a gleaming eye could spy through in the far right bottom corner of the pane. The next time Stephanie went in the bathroom I hurried outside and mounted my ladder. Disappointingly, though, she had not come to shower but to brush her teeth and pee. I didn't get to see much of anything. Standing sideways to me, she yanked down her pants and underpants and squatted down on the toilet in one quick, continuous motion. It seemed to me she sat strangely far forward on the toilet, more as though riding a horse. And then after a moment came a surprising amount of dabbing at herself as she reached again and again to rip off more sheets of pink toilet paper. When she flushed the toilet, she was still sitting upon it. Finally, just as I was about to get my first glimpse of her butt in profile, she raised her head and her eyes came sweeping up and I had to duck away, afraid she might spot me.

Her next visit to the bathroom was more like it. When I pressed my eye to the glass she was already stepping out of her clothes. I got a good, straight-on look at her body as she gathered her hair back behind her head and sauntered toward the tub. She really was a little princess. Now that she was finally nude I could see just how proudly erect she carried herself. Her body was rounder, softer, than Kimberly's, though just as hairless, and I liked the color of her body: white, but a warmer, better white than the milky, too-white whiteness of me and my family.

From my vantage point high above the bathtub I could see only the top of her head as she showered, but the reward for my patience came when she pushed back the shower curtain and climbed out, her flushed, high little butt visible for long moments at a time as she toweled herself, concentrating on her hair. When she'd at last finished buffing it, her hair fell long and glossy, all the way down to the top of her crack.

The odd thing is that for me there were almost two Stephanies now. When I was with her, doing the ways, I never thought about this other, naked-body Stephanie that I spied upon.

Mesmerized as I was by Stephanie, I told my father that I wasn't interested in going along on the annual summer car trip to Cleveland. And so Dad and my brother and sister hit the road without me. But not long after they'd driven off an agony of regret came over me. The trip I'd scorned now seemed like a magical adventure I'd denied myself; it was unbearable to think I'd made an irreversible decision. But when I told my mother how I felt she unexpectedly took pity on me and said, in a voice rising with excitement: "Honey, what if I put you on a bus tonight? You could be there in the morning. They'd all come pick you up at the bus station with your little suitcase. I could call Daddy tonight and tell him when to expect you." Mom cackled a delighted laugh. She'd always loved dramatic plans conceived and acted upon out of the blue.

Stephanie and her little brother and sister said they didn't want to come along to drop me off downtown at the bus station. Though I was the one leaving her, I felt hurt by Stephanie's indifference. A moment later, though, as we were heading out, she suddenly ran into the bedroom (with my sister gone, the room was all hers) and slammed the door shut behind her.

The three hundred and fifty miles of interstate highway between Chicago and Cleveland had added up, with family pit stops, to an eight-hour car trip that we must have made, it seemed, about a million times during my childhood. As I got older the ride never got any less excruciating or endless. The trip began with the mildly diverting Chicago Skyway, a long, steadily climbing ascent into Indiana that invariably made us kids roll up the windows against the sulfur stench of the Gary steel mills and laugh about someone having trouble controlling their farting. After this excitement there was nothing but dull flat landscape accompanying us all the way to Cleveland: cornfields, soybean fields, cow pasture. Somewhere near South Bend, Dad would never fail to point out the barn side with a giant white "A's" painted on it that belonged to the eccentric and famously cheap Charlie Finley, owner of the Oakland Athletics baseball team. But even if someone had had something more interesting to say, the roar inside our Volkswagen station wagon (loud engine, windows wide open) discouraged conversation by making you have to yell above the din. And so I'd fall into a stupefied half-sleep in the rear of the car above the hot, noisy, pulsating engine that only Volkswagen, apparently, thought to place in the back of its cars to torture kids. Just when I'd think I could take no more, the trailer parks of Toledo would appear on the left side of the highway and I'd know that Grandma and Grandpa's Fowl Farm was still a hundred miles away.

For all the tedium of these trips, I'd been happily secure—so secure, it never bore thinking about—in my right to feel what I felt, do what I did, be where I was, and exist like millions of other kids on the long, boring road to Grandma and Grandpa's. But now aboard my unexpected Greyhound bus, I began to feel increasingly uneasy. At first I'd been occupied with the novelty of traveling this overly familiar road at night. And I'd thought of Stephanie, of course. I indulged myself in the new pleasure of missing someone, and as the bus sped through the night I stared at my very serious-looking reflection in the dark window and imagined that Stephanie missed me too, that she regretted not coming to see me off. But when we pulled into Toledo deep in the night there came a long, unscheduled delay at the station, and my thoughts turned to Dad and the Cleveland relatives. We were going to be almost two hours late getting into Cleveland but I had no idea how to go about making a collect call or even how to get ahold of Grandma and Grandpa Fleming's telephone number. All my life I'd been a dutiful kid who'd racked up near-perfect grades and attendance in grade school, and it was only in a few bad dreams that I ever experienced the sinking feeling of being in the wrong place at the wrong time—showing up outside the school doors at midnight, for instance, having somehow missed the big test given earlier that day.

To feel myself suddenly out of sync with things in real life—well, this was the real nightmare. My mad trip to Cleveland now had the distinct air of something not meant to be. Sure enough, later that morning in Cleveland Dad was far from thrilled to see me and seemed very irritated that I'd decided to show up like this. Grandma and Grandpa Fleming acted strangely distant, as though they disapproved of me. Now I realize that what they disapproved of must have been my mother—her having divorced and, as they saw it, betrayed my dad. For them, Mom's sending me on this crazy bus ride must have counted as but one more example of her overall craziness these past few years. But because I was still too young to grasp such a serpentine adult practice as penalizing a boy for being his mother's stand-in, I took the cold reception in Cleveland personally and couldn't wait to get back to Chicago and Stephanie. Grandma and Grandpa's Fowl Farm, which had been such a wonderful extension of my world all through childhood, was never again a very friendly place for me.

The worst part of the summer was still to come. Late in August Ricki announced that she and the kids were going home to Northbrook. It had been a wonderful summer, Ricki told me, and she particularly appreciated how I'd served as a "great role model" for her son, Stevie. She only hoped he'd grow up to be half as nice as I. But now there was the kids' upcoming school year to think about—Stephanie, for instance, would be entering junior high and they needed to find out what kind of supplies she'd be expected to have.

I was totally shocked. I'd never regarded their stay with us as anything temporary. One of the summer's charms, in fact, had been the lack of any sense of the future—of the fall, of school, of what would become of me and Stephanie.

Their home in Northbrook lay about twelve miles away from our house in Evanston—quite a long ways for a twelve year old boy on a bicycle. If it's true that the typical male response to anything distressing is to take action, any course of action, rather than give way to brooding, then I was being very male when I set out on my bike one morning, feeling determined to go to heroic lengths to keep Stephanie in my life. I'd telephoned her to see if it was okay that I visited, and Stephanie must not have been used to talking on the phone because she sounded very distant as she said it was okay. It was mid-afternoon when I pedaled up to their large white ranch house, thirsty and exhausted from having gotten lost several times. Stephanie greeted me with odd formality at the front door. She looked the same, the same shiny curtain of hair, but she acted as though we hadn't just spent the summer doing the ways together. In the large, basement rec room she slipped behind a full walnut bar that stood in one corner and poured me a Coke in a highball glass stuffed with ice cubes. I kept waiting for her strange new manner to melt but her idea of how to spend this precious, hard-won time together was to squander it on a long desultory game of pool. Her mother, Ricki, was nowhere to be seen, nor was there any sign of her father, the mysterious Dr. Kim, whom I'd never met and wasn't sure I wanted to meet. Perhaps it was his sense of formality that I was seeing in Stephanie now and in the anonymous, hotel-lobby ambiance of the house.

After our pointless game of pool it was already time to set off on the long ride home. I climbed on my bike and Stephanie, finally friendly, said, "Wouldn't it be great if you had a motor- cycle and we could go places together?" This put me in great spirits until I realized, a mile or so down the road, that it would be four long years before I could get a driver's license, let alone a motorcycle. And so with every block I pedaled past I became more and more resigned to the Kims and their house in North- brook just being too far away.

PHOTO BY DON DASKAIS

Mom and the Free School

The story of how I got to be in such a bad way that Uncle Eddie felt he had to rescue me begins with what seemed like a big favor my mother did for me. Early in September, just as I was about to enter seventh grade, Mom told me about a "neat new school" she'd heard about. It was called the Evanston Free School and a bunch of local parents, fed up with the "mindless rote learning" of the public schools, were starting it up in the basement of the Unitarian church our family sometimes attended. "How would you like to go there, sugar?" my mother asked me. Quickly, guiltily, I said yes, sure, I would. From the little Mom told me, I got the idea it would almost be like not attending school at all. The Free School had no grades or rules of any kind and kids could apparently do whatever they liked.

The Free School, I sensed, was my mother's way of compensating me for the pain of the past two years. Of us three kids, I'd taken the ups and downs and movings around the hardest. The first time Mom and Dad decided to separate, for instance, it made my head spin. We were all in the car coming home from the beach one day, I remember, when my mother turned around in the front seat and gave us the shocking news. When she got to the part about us kids moving with her to an apartment on the South Side of Chicago, it was like hearing my life was ending. Flashing before my eyes was the image of my elementary school grounds—the oak trees, my friends playing, this little green world that was the only one that mattered to me—now falling further and further below as I was swept off into the clouds.

I was so freaked out that my parents ended up deciding I would remain with Dad in the Evanston house while my brother and sister went off to live with Mom. Though divorce became commonplace just a few years later, my parents' separation in 1969 was still such a big deal that the mother of one of my friends, hearing the news, actually invited me over for a special lunch where she treated me as carefully as though I'd just been diagnosed with leukemia.

For a few months my father and I ate hamburger dinners and I saw my mother, brother, and sister on weekend visits. But one Sunday my mother decided to "kidnap" me, as she jokingly put it, because she wanted all three of her kids living with her. I found it so far from a laughing matter, however, that I told her dead seriously, "I want to call my lawyer." In the tiny one-bedroom apartment she'd rented near the University of Chicago campus in Hyde Park, my little brother and I slept in one twin bed, my sister in the other, while Mom took the couch in the living room. A couple blocks down the street stood my new, ominous-looking elementary school where Mom had found a job teaching the first grade. My first day there I remember standing in gym class and watching freight cars lumbering past on the elevated tracks just outside the towering grilled windows of the old gymnasium. For a sheltered suburban kid like me it felt almost like I'd been put in a reformatory.

One morning we kids woke up and found Dad, not Mom, in the living room. He said our mother loved us all very much but that she was having some problems right now, and needed time by herself to rest. We asked where she was and he said we'd talk about that later, once she got her situation sorted out. Then he took us back to Evanston with him.

Soon it came out that Mom was back in the hospital. But though Dad took to acting distracted and tense, and though the very formal Jamaican woman he'd hired to cook meals for us, Mrs. Jacks, never stopped seeming like a stranger in our house, it was not until the following spring, when we set out on a family car trip to Cleveland without Mom, that the weight of her absence really caught up with me. We'd barely crossed over the Chicago Skyway when a wet heavy snow began falling. Though it was early April, the snow kept coming down thicker and thicker. The highway ahead of us was becoming whited out and emptied of other cars and yet my father drove grimly on, our speed shrinking to thirty miles an hour, to twenty, to ten. For what seemed an eternity he resisted the reality that we'd landed in the middle of a paralyzing blizzard. His thinking seemed to be that because these things weren't supposed to happen in April, they didn't happen; we were just going to ride this freak thing out because any minute it had to be ending. Everything my father had achieved in life had been thanks to his plodding perseverance (my mother told me he'd set some sort of record by taking nine years to earn his Ph.D.), but this inability of his to respond to the unexpected, to the bizarre, to the hopeless—well, it was a fitting allegory for his whole experience with my mother.

At last even Dad had to accept that the road was becoming impassable. We creaked off the highway when an exit presented itself and found ourselves inching along the Main Street of a tiny Indiana town. Fortunately, a diner was open: Betty's Fine Foods. It's a name we've never forgotten because we ended up spending the day marooned in there. The Beatles song "Let It

Be" had just come out and on the little jukebox attached to our booth in Betty's we must have played "Let It Be" a hundred times as we sat there, the only customers, waiting out the snow.

I'd taken the last two Beatles hits very personally because each seemed to be an uncanny commentary on the state of our family. Their song "Come Together" had been on the radio all the time the past fall in Hyde Park when my mother "kidnapped" me; not only the chorus ("Come together! right now, over me"), but the moody atmosphere of the song, its bass line full of forboding, had spoken to and explored the aching feelings in my stomach. Now in Betty's Fine Foods, as "Let It Be" played on and on, the song seemed to be giving the funeral rites for family life as we'd known it, its melancholy resignation piling up on us like the snow still coming down hard. The day had become one long dirge. It was just all very sad.

My parents made one last stab at making their marriage work when Mom got out of the hospital later that spring. With their arms slung around each other, Mom and Dad walked us kids to school one morning and I guess there was supposed to be a feeling of triumph in the air. We're a family again, kids! But I couldn't quite suspend my disbelief. Sure enough, by Christmas Mom was back in the hospital again. Three months after that, she and Dad divorced.

The habits of a young life are not thrown away overnight and it took some time for the Free School to erode my self-discipline, my guilt. The first few mornings I raced to the bus stop, afraid to be late. At nine o'clock sharp I'd be hurrying down the steps of the Free School's separate entrance: a concrete stairwell descending to an underground connecting tunnel that always made me feel I was entering a bomb shelter, not a church basement. I discovered that early in the morning nothing much was ever going on at the school; most students and teachers showed up only after ten-thirty or eleven. But if it felt wrong to linger at home by myself half the morning, it also felt wrong to linger around the deserted Free School doing nothing. The compromise I ended up reaching with myself was that so long as I arrived at school "on time," as I still thought of it, I could then permit myself to go off on long solitary rambles around the surrounding area. But later in the morning, when everyone else had finally straggled into school, I found myself drifting in for only the briefest appearances before heading outside again for more of my long walks. I kept expecting one of the teachers to pull me aside and ask what I was doing disappearing all the time. But no one told me anything.

I didn't know it then but the Free School's guiding philosophy was the romantic notion of Father Free School himself, A. S. Neill, the founder of the Summerhill School in England, that children are innately wise about their educational needs. So wise, it seemed, that the role of teachers was simply to serve their wunderkinder, not direct them. But this enormous respect for a student's self-direction meant that a shy kid like me was left to wander around like an unnoticed little ghost. I guess everyone assumed I had no interest in taking part in classes. As I drifted further and further into my own little world, no one dared to interfere.

The odd thing was that a year earlier I'd been guiltily slinking off these same church grounds. My father had enrolled me in the Unitarian church's Sunday school whose classes were conducted in the same underground cinderblock rooms that the Free School now operated out of. Each Sunday morning when Dad dropped me off in front of the church with a quarter to take the bus home afterward, I'd wait for his car to drive off and then slip away. I'd use the quarter to buy chocolate cupcakes that I ate while roaming through the snowy, sleepy Sunday streets before making the long walk home. It was the first time I'd ever played hooky from anything. Even after I became confident that my absences were not being reported to my father, I always felt a twinge of uneasiness about sneaking around like this. On the other hand, these stolen hours of freedom each Sunday morning were a sweet new feeling for a kid who'd always done as he was told.

Now here I was at the Free School playing hooky full-time. Soon the vast empty freedom I'd entered began to be filled with music. Lurking in the school hallway one morning I happened to hear an old Beatles record playing away and I stood there entranced. I bought the album *Meet the Beatles* that day, and my new morning routine became listening to the melancholy ballad "This Boy" just one more time on our big mahogany stereo before setting off for school. Soon I had all their early albums because Beatles music functioned as the perfect soundtrack for my solitude; the songs, as I heard them, seemed written in an effort to raise some warmth against the cold. In an enchanted ballad such as "Nowhere Man," for instance, the background vocals, the "Ah, la-la-la" 's, always made me think of the meager warmth a car's heater puts out on a winter night's drive.

Before long I knew the songs so well I could play them in my head during all the hours and hours I devoted to rambling along a magical road, Ridge Avenue, that swept past the school. Ridge ran along an actual ridge that, in the otherwise flat prairie landscape of Evanston, had captured my imagination from the first time I laid eyes on it as a little kid being ferried along its distinctive road bed that was often sunk down several feet below the high bank rising up on one side. To be exploring the wonder of Ridge on foot now, walking the high spine of its bank that a retaining wall of long thin stones stacked like piles of books kept from crumbling down into the road—well, I never tired of it. I'd shamble along munching cupcakes, lost in a poetic haze of "Nowhere Man" and "This Boy." Every so often I'd turn around and retrace my steps so that several times a day I could be seen passing and re-passing the concrete hulk of the Unitarian church and its flying wedges like huge slices of bread coming out of a toaster tipped over on its side. By late November the somber architecture of bare tree branches had emerged overhead. By December snowflakes whipped against my feet as I stood on the bottom step of one of the little flights of stone stairs cut into the bank. And if you'd told me then that I was on my way to becoming so weird that I'd end up in a mental hospital, I never could have believed it.

My mother had no idea how I was spending my time at the Free School, for unlike other parents she never stopped by the school or attended any of the Tuesday night meetings. She had only the vaguest impression, I think, of the place being full of children's rights. When she mentioned the Free School at all, it would be when she was angry with me for moaning that I'd take the garbage out later, not now. Then she'd threaten to withhold the tuition check she paid the school each month. And so though the details of my new life eluded her, she had grasped one essential reality: I'd do anything not to return to public school.

My mother's disengagement from me was due to how busy she'd become—that fall she was attending her first semester of graduate school, working as a counselor at the very psychiatric hospital where she'd been a patient nine months earlier, and going to Alcoholics Anonymous meetings three times a week. My own obliviousness to her, however, had no basis except daydreaminess. I was so out of it that I made a shocking discovery about Mom only thanks to a neighborhood friend. He and I happened to walk into our house one evening to find the living room filled with strange women. The AA group Mom had joined was an all-woman chapter and this was her turn to host the group. My friend was just as surprised as I by the festive, smoky scene and after we'd said awkward hellos all around, we two boys went into the kitchen, closing the door behind us.

"What's your mom doing with all those dykes out there?" my friend asked me. Though he was my age, twelve, his breath smelled of Kool cigarettes that he stole from his dad. His family was the closest thing we had to hillbillies on the block and their name, appropriately, was the Hills. His dad had a glass eye and a T-shirt always grimed with grease from tinkering with the motorcycles he kept sprawled out all over their backyard. His mom, as my own mother loved to point out, was always padding around the house in dirty bare feet.

My friend's tone suggested I should feel embarrassed about

the new company my mother was keeping, but I felt only flus-
tered by my lack of knowledge. "I don't know," I told him. "This
is the first time I've ever seen them."

"Oh yeah? Ever wonder if your mom's a dyke now too?"

Later, as Mom emptied the ashtrays and collected the coffee
cups, I brought up my friend's questions, politely remembering
to substitute *gay* for *dyke*. Mom sighed, had us both sit down,
and then adopted the same portentous tone she'd used to tell
me the truth about Uncle Eddie. "Well, honey, I guess that's
something I'm in the process of figuring out right now."

This process had in fact been going on right under my nose
the whole time Ricki and her kids had been staying with us. For
while I was busy spying on Stephanie in the bathroom and doing
"the ways" with her in the attic, Mom and Ricki had been having
a summerlong affair. Each night after we kids went to bed, the
two mothers would treat themselves to a midnight candlelight
dinner followed by a long stroll around our sleepy suburban
neighborhood arm in arm. For appearances' sake, Ricki insisted
on ending the night alone on the living room couch.

There was one more surprise: my mother's fling with Ricki
was not her first gay experience. A few years earlier Mom had
had a brief affair with a housewife down the block, a woman
who happened to be the mother of Kimberly, the girl who used
to strip for me in the attic. And so, in a connection between my
mother and me I never could have imagined, the two girls I'd
fooled around with—Kimberly and Stephanie—were daughters
of the two women Mom had been involved with.

In the end my mother's news was more curious than shocking
to me. The rule of thumb, I've heard, is that it's the child of
the same sex who takes the gay parent's homosexuality much
more to heart, and this was certainly the case in our family (it
was a much bigger deal for my sister, when she eventually heard
about it, than for my little brother and me). I soon settled into
pretty much the same attitude regarding Mom that I took toward Uncle Eddie's being gay. For I never spent any time imag-

ining the actual physicality of lesbian sex, even when a few months later I happened to overhear my mother going at it with her new girlfriend. Mom had met Phyllis through one of the members of her all-woman AA group. "Phyl" was pretty, petite, and Italian American and had the inexhaustible bland cheerfulness of a small-time newscaster. My mother said it drove her crazy the way Phyl would strike up long conversations with any stranger she came across—a garage man, an old lady walking her dog. It took all of us the longest time to realize this was Phyl's genuine personality and not something she put on.

I overheard them making love when I happened to wake up one night at two in the morning needing to go to the bathroom. In our little house the one bathroom was downstairs, next to what used to be my parents' bedroom. As I passed this bedroom's closed door, I could hear my mother—or was it Phyl?—intimately moaning, "Yes, oh yes!" But by the time I'd climbed back in bed I'd put the whole thing behind me. It was no more unsettling for me than overhearing my parents doing it would have been, since parental sexuality of any kind struck me as gross and hardly something to dwell upon.

My mother gave much of the credit for her "resurrection" to Uncle Eddie. He'd encouraged her to think big, and when she'd told him her fantasy was to become a psychiatric social worker he lent her thousands of dollars so she could go back to school. And he was the one who'd gotten her into AA. Unlike the staff at Mom's various bughouses who'd all told her that her drinking was only a symptom of her personal problems, Eddie convinced Mom that her drinking itself was the main problem. His role in her sexual direction, though, was much trickier. For years his own homosexuality had struck my mother as so embarrassing and weird that you could almost say I have Uncle Eddie to thank for my very existence, since my mother's determination to be as normal and as different from him as possible made marriage and children seem like the best answer. But now, in the do-your-own-thing 1970s, it was a whole new story. The more glamorous example Eddie had been setting since he moved to New York also must have helped my mother decide to take the big plunge.

The next time we saw Uncle Eddie, during a Christmas visit in 1972, I'd become a different kid. At thirteen I was now heavily into Bob Dylan. I'd taken over the classical guitar Mom had stopped playing years ago and spent hours writing songs up in my attic room. I was in my second year at the Free School and my thick hair, catching up in shagginess with the other Free School kids', fell messily to my shoulders. More important, I'd finally gotten into the swing of things at school and had a new pack of friends with big houses where I slept over for nights at a time. I never bothered calling home to check in because my mother was hardly ever home herself, finding it easier to spend the night at Phyl's apartment down in the city. When I heard Uncle Eddie say that "friends are the witnesses to our lives" it made perfect sense to me because my family had stopped being people I talked to or even saw very much.

Most of my new friends lived in wealthy south Evanston near the lake in houses that seemed all the bigger for there being no fathers in them. With so many floors and bathrooms and stair-cases, domestic life was lighter-hearted and vaguer, it seemed to me. These sprawling Victorian homes absorbed me and other freeloaders so effortlessly that I rarely ran into the mothers of the children who lived in them. In the house I stayed over at most often the mother was stunningly beautiful. I was friends with her younger son, a boy who had her ringleted, dark-brown hair. In his huge bedroom four or five of us would sit up late at night in beanbag chairs, passing around a water bong and then passing out till morning. Our twelve-year-old host could afford to be generous with his marijuana because each month his father out in California mailed a generous child support check directly to him in the belief that taking charge of his own finances would instill a sense of responsibility in the boy.

Another of my new friends was a boy who, like me, lived in modest northwest Evanston. He and I would make the trek to our south Evanston friends' houses on foot together, sometimes setting out so late that the city's ten P.M. curfew had gone into effect, forcing us to take a clandestine route that kept us out of sight of roaming police squad cars. First there was the long dark corridor of interconnected, graveled alleyways we'd discovered; next, when we thought the coast was clear of cops, the scary dash across a brilliant boulevard. Then we were home free. Crashing through the tangled underbrush, we'd make our way along the bank of the sanitary canal, the murky waterway running through the heart of north Evanston, until we reached the Chicago & Northwestern Railroad tracks. These unlighted tracks, running high above street level on their own man-made bank, served as our secret express line to south Evanston, letting us cross the city while remaining invisible to the cops below.

It was a lot of fun, this life. I had all the wild freedoms of an alley cat without any of the usual price to pay. Or so it seemed.

Yet when I saw Uncle Eddie again eight months later, I'd become more serious—become a communist, in fact. A new teacher at the Free School had a straightforwardness that was particularly effective with me. All this time, it turned out, I'd been waiting to be *enrolled* into something, anything, by someone confident that he knew what I needed. From the moment Simon introduced himself to me by clapping me heartily on the back and asking, then insisting, I join a class—"a political class"—he was starting up, I'd found him hard to resist. Still, I hadn't known quite what to make of him until I heard another teacher, a woman, say: "I can see why Simon's so popular with students: he's got looks, brains, and loads of charisma." Suddenly I was very impressed with Simon. In a school full of dowdy earth shoes and winter coats puffy with goose down, Simon strode around in an old army field jacket and enormous combat boots. At six-four he towered over everyone and when I learned he'd run on the track team in college I kept expecting his powerful figure, bent forward with hurry as he rushed through the school each morning with giant strides, to break into a gallop.

Simon often arrived just in time for class because his car, a battered green Datsun, was always breaking down. On his tiny salary of twenty-five hundred dollars a year he would have to wait weeks before he could afford to have the car repaired, making him have to hitchhike in each morning from his rented room just across the Chicago border in Roger's Park. The minute he burst into the Free School we, his eight or nine students, would all scurry after him into the cloakroom we used as a classroom. There Simon would already have begun the business of freeing himself from his capacious field jacket whose many pockets we'd learned were stuffed with "literature," as he called all his leaflets advertising upcoming rallies and boycotts and meetings.

At the beginning of class I'd find myself staring in fascination at Simon's neck, which would be flushed a bright, raw red. Was it windburn? Perhaps such a vigorous man got impatient with waiting alongside Sheridan Road for a ride and simply ran the three miles to school, neck exposed to the stinging wind off Lake Michigan. Or could it be that his skin was so sensitive that the act of morning shaving set it aflame? Maybe this was it because though Simon was pure guerrilla below the shoulders, above them he was complicated, intellectual, even nerdy. His distinctive cap of lank, glossy hair, a blend of brown and copper that he parted far over to one side, had long bangs that came sweeping over the tops of his heavy black glasses. He'd just graduated from Northwestern University the past spring but it was impossible to think of him as being only twenty-two or -three; his confidence and convictions made him seem years older.

That class so often started with Simon heaving for breath went together in my mind with the breathless urgency of his message; there clearly wasn't a moment to lose in his instruction of us. He'd named his class U.S. Imperialism because I think his original plan had been to use American exploitation of the Third World as a gentle starting point for working up to his real agenda—turning us all into Maoist revolutionaries. But once he got going in the cloakroom/classroom he must have found it impossible to contain himself because I can't recall my conversion to communism taking any time. I never had the sense I was imbibing a controversial ideology; rather, it seemed that Simon was teaching us something self-evident and elementary, along the lines of the laws of physics. My only concern was whether I could absorb it all. There was so much to learn!

Soon we were off on a field trip to a left-wing bookstore in the city where we each purchased a copy of *Quotations from Chairman Mao*, the distinctive Little Red Book. Flipping my copy open, I peeled back the piece of protective tissue and unveiled a disappointing color portrait of Mao Tse-tung, my first glimpse of the Chairman, whose name (was it his last or his first?) I'd learned to pronounce *say dung*. That his face was utterly ordinary and unheroic was disappointing enough but it also looked as though a bit of rouge had been daubed on his cheeks. I wondered if I'd really find in him the same magic I'd found in idols such as the Beatles and Bob Dylan.

Just as I'd feared, the Little Red Book wasn't too good a read. The real genius of the book was its portability, and though I stopped reading it, I carried it around with me everywhere like a wallet. My most exciting moment with *Quotations from Chairman Mao*, though, occurred the night that I lost it when a policeman stopped me on the street for violating the town curfew. He eventually let me go, but not before frisking me and yelping in surprise at finding the Little Red Book, which he promptly confiscated. After he'd driven off in his squad car I felt thrilled and proud to tell others I'd horrified the authorities. Still, I never got around to replacing my copy.

Because Simon was determined that we students avoid stagnating in mere "rhetoric," cold Saturday mornings would find us milling around supermarket parking lots, picketing on behalf of Cesar Chavez's striking farmworkers and chanting at incoming shoppers to boycott the grapes and iceberg lettuce that had been picked by nonunion scabs. On Sundays, when I saw my father, I'd try my hand at radicalizing him, even though it was pretty apparent that Dad was a hopeless liberal. A "liberal," as I knew now from Simon's teachings, was not a person with progressive views but rather a middle-class stooge who believed capitalism could be made kinder and gentler. Still, each Sunday I'd harangue Dad for hours about the looming inevitability of violent class struggle and proletarian revolution. He'd always hear me out with a silence that bordered on absentmindedness; Dad was so quiet, in fact, that I began to wish he'd interrupt and contest me because that would at least mean I'd succeeded in denting his calm if not his beliefs.

But what my father's silence obscured from me was how great an achievement it had been for him to *escape* the proletariat. He and his brothers had all taken advantage of cheap state colleges to better themselves, entering professional lives and buying homes that, unlike their childhood farmhouse, were not hooked up to a crude well beneath the house that delivered brackish, nearly undrinkable water. American capitalism had worked sensationally well for my father. And unlike Simon, whose British-born parents were quite wealthy, my father knew working-class life too intimately to romanticize it. The spur that drove him on through college more than anything, in fact, was the prospect of a life at the Ford plant he toiled in each summer to pay for his studies.

But none of this had occurred to me at that time and so my failure to indoctrinate my dad depressed me; it reminded me how much I still had to learn. Embarrassingly, I wasn't even sure whether I was a Maoist or a Marxist-Leninist, a socialist or a communist. I doubted these terms could really be as interchangeable as Simon's talks seemed to imply, but wasn't Marx himself, confusingly, a socialist? And was I the only one who had no idea what "dialectical materialism" meant?

Yes, I had lots of studying to do but it never entered my mind that Simon would ever question my "commitment." Yet that's what happened at the end of the school year. Simon had organized a weekend retreat for U.S. Imperialism class at his parents' summer home on the Michigan side of Lake Michigan, resort country, and as we lounged together on the hard-packed sand of the little private beach, I happened to tell him that it would be cool to get as skinny as Dylan and have an old refrigerator like he did that was empty except for some weird stuff growing in it.

Instantly, Simon's forceful hand was crushing my fingers together with real outrage. "What's *with* you? That's being part of the *problem*! Is that what you want? To be like that . . . that sexist, counterproductive pig?"

It hadn't occurred to me that Dylan and Maoism were incompatible. On the contrary, I'd been able to see a certain kinship between my blue Mao cap and the black corduroy one I thought of as my Dylan hobo cap. But now it appeared that Dylan and the Beatles and also my own songs were all "decadent" as well as "bourgeois," and that Maoism—stern, moral Maoism—laid claim to every corner of me.

Having just turned fourteen, I wasn't too sure I was ready to martyr the rest of my life to the Cause. All summer, away from Simon, I struggled with the question as I worked in the hot, deserted church. The minister had asked if I wanted a summer job and now for weeks and weeks I painted walls, cleaned out gutters, swept, mopped, and waxed the floors. The boredom and loneliness of it were excruciating but in the end my reward was what seemed to me a mountain of money. But I was weak. Though Simon and communism still seemed irrefutable, I couldn't resist indulging the decadent part of me by buying a beautiful steel-string guitar. With my remaining money, I decided to take the train to New York and visit Uncle Eddie.

I guess I was looking for answers but what I found in New York wasn't anything I expected. It was late August and I didn't know that the city was half-empty because everyone who could afford to had fled the heat. My uncle's latest apartment was in Greenwich Village, way over by the Hudson River at the far end of Horatio Street. To reach it Donny, the long-haired Free School friend who'd accompanied me, and I had to pass through the meat-packing district with its sickening reek of fresh blood. This still didn't prepare the two of us for the filthy, sticky stairwell and battered apartment doors of my uncle's building as we climbed up toward his welcoming voice on the third floor. Inside his tiny studio apartment, which smelled of books and cigarettes and coffee grounds, it was almost like being in a jail cell with all the burglar bars on the windows. The apartment was so tiny that Uncle Eddie went off to a friend's for the night, leaving us boys to sleep there by ourselves.

The next day my uncle took us up to the Cloisters at the surprisingly unspoiled tip of Manhattan. He'd brought along a tall friend who, so my uncle confided to me and Donny afterward, found our little outing to have been "the best day of his life." It seemed like a strange comment to make about a pretty ho-hum day plodding around the Cloisters and its grounds. Much more fun for me and Donny was another friend of my uncle's who spent hours showing us around town. This funny man, Ray, had the style of an overgrown teenager, for he was just as careless about his appearance as Donny and I were, going around with his shirttails hanging out and a ponytail flopping against his back. But he had a mock-exasperated manner ("*Now what!*") that encouraged, and was probably designed to encourage, us two boys to act impertinent around him. Donny and I worried we'd gone too far, though, when we repeated to Ray what Uncle Eddie had told us—that Ray, who claimed to be a vegetarian, never actually ate vegetables and could more accurately be called a "candy-atarian." As Ray reacted with a look of comic seething, he made us burst out laughing by exclaiming, "Oh, that uncle of yours!"

Perhaps my uncle had paid Ray some baby-sitter's money to take us around town for long stretches of the day. Ray certainly was at our service. Hearing that I idolized Bob Dylan, he marched us over to Gerde's Folk City on West Third Street, the club where Dylan had played in his early days. Disappointingly, the legendary place now stood next to a McDonald's. Ray then walked us over to an ivied brownstone where he said Dylan had lived until just recently. "A very nasty drunk, I hear," he said, pursing his lips with either distaste or amusement, I couldn't tell which.

This little Dylan tour had definitely tarnished his legend a bit for me but what I really needed to hear was something, anything, that would help me resolve what to do about Maoism. My uncle was curiously mum on the subject. A few years later he would tell me he felt he didn't dare weigh in on it, even though he himself was a socialist of sorts. Instead it was left to yet another of his friends to put Maoism in a whole new light for me. "The real trouble with communism," this man said very casually, "is just that it's so *boring*."

Yet that fall when I began my third year at the Free School I quickly got caught up with Simon all over again. It was the father void in my life, I suppose, that made him mean so much to me. My Maoism had always been less an ideological commitment than a personal allegiance to Simon and I guess I probably would have followed him into anything he happened to espouse—Hare Krishna, heroin, terrorism. So it was one thing to find Maoism too much, quite another to walk away from this flesh-and-blood hero in my life. One day, however, Simon showed up at school with a shockingly short haircut that was painful to look at because it made him seem diminished, even humiliated. But his scalping turned out to be part of a plan he'd hatched. He would soon be leaving the Free School, he told us, to take a job at a steel mill in Gary, Indiana, where he could "work from within the system"—work to bring the system down, that is, by infiltrating the rank-and-file workers and gradually fomenting their dissent. The haircut would help him pass himself off as just one of the guys. Soon Simon was urging us students to reenter the system as well—the public school system, in our case. But though I'd begun to feel that it was probably time to leave the Free School, this was more from a sense of growing out of step with the outside world, of being someone who's stayed too long in a weird little cult. I couldn't really see myself spreading the word about communism at Evanston High.

And then, during our last real talk together, Simon dropped a bomb on me that killed my Maoism once and for all. We were riding along in his Datsun, just the two of us, and I remember how excited Simon got when Helen Reddy's new song "I Am Woman" came on the car radio. "*Listen* to that!" he kept exclaiming as the lyrics unfolded ("I am Woman, hear me roar, in numbers too big to ignore"). It thrilled him to think the American public was being radicalized over the AM airwaves. But a few minutes later, as I was musing to him about the future, I started to say something like, "As a member of the proletariat, I'll—" when Simon interrupted to tell me irritably that I could never be part of "the people," as he called the proletariat, because I was and always would be culturally middle class. "People like us can't be part of the revolutionary vanguard," he said. "Our job is just to help fan the flames."

I'm sure Simon had no idea how disheartening I found this news. It managed to touch on the two things I feared most: that I could never really belong, and that I would be excluded from glory. My whole soul balked at such a static scheme of things because the possibility of self-transformation was what I was living for. What I found most thrilling about Bob Dylan's story was that this Minnesota college dropout named Bobby Zimmerman whom no one thought was all that special had, in a very short time, completely on his own, with an eerie confidence unsupported by anything the surrounding world was telling him, as though struck by the most unlikely lightning, morphed into Bob Dylan.

That Christmas Uncle Eddie and I had our best and longest talk ever. By the end of it we'd all but decided I would come and live with him in New York. My uncle had flown into town on Christmas Eve and then rushed around O'Hare Airport buying books and chocolates and perfume, having forgotten to bring any presents with him. He was staying downtown with my grandmother Delilah in her Marina Towers apartment on the fifty-eighth floor. The rest of us family—my mother, brother, sister, and I—joined them for Christmas dinner. While my mother, who'd recently had her slipped disk operated on, lay out flat on my grandmother's thick white rug, Uncle Eddie told us about an eccentric Connecticut family who'd called him up one night and talked to him for more than an hour about his recently published first novel, *Forgetting Elena:* "I guess the mother had discovered *Forgetting Elena* at their local library and she liked it so much that she made the rest of the family, even the little kids, read it. Then, as if this wasn't enough, she decided they should all personally thank the author. So she looked up my number and put everyone on the line with me in turns. Some of the kids couldn't have been more than ten or eleven but they'd be telling me in these polite little voices, 'Uh, Mr. White, I just wanted to say that I especially enjoyed the scene where Herbert and your protagonist compose rhymed triplets.' "

As the evening wore on my mother and grandmother launched into family stories I'd heard a hundred times before, and I got restless. I told everyone I was going home by myself on the El train but my grandmother, looking gravely alarmed, said it wasn't safe to be out alone at this time of night in the city. This seemed so ridiculous to me: Did she have no idea I'd been traveling around on my own at all hours for over a year now? I was about to leave anyway, storming out if necessary, when Uncle Eddie said he'd ride the El with me back to Evanston. This, however, got my mother going. She told Eddie she had lots of things to talk to him about "one-on-one" and that if it was so important we leave right away, then why didn't we all just drive back to Evanston together in the car? But this only got my grandmother going. Christmas is supposed to be family time, she said. Why didn't everyone just calm down and have another helping of pumpkin pie? In the end it impressed me how smoothly yet firmly Uncle Eddie eased us both out the door, telling my grandmother he'd be back tomorrow to take her out for a nice long lunch before his flight to New York, telling my mother he needed to get some air and stretch his legs, that in New York they weren't used to being cooped up in cars all the time, that this way he could spend some time with me and then still talk to her back in Evanston all night if she liked.

Uncle Eddie and I made our way up snowy State Street, crossing over the Chicago River now permanently green from all the times it had been dyed for St. Patrick's Day. He told me that when he was my age, living in Evanston with my mother and grandmother, he'd often ridden the El at night, sometimes in this same situation when "family life just became something I needed to escape for a while." My uncle seemed so much the New Yorker that it was hard to picture him ever living in Evanston. Sure enough, a minute later he was pointing out to me that whereas in Manhattan the streets were always thronged with people, "in Chicago even the biggest intersections, like State and Wacker here, will often have just this one old black man walking around with a bunch of pigeons flying overhead."

My uncle had a knack for saying things that lodged themselves in my memory. Earlier that night, for instance, he'd said, "Oh, I see . . . the Poor Boy look—very nice," when he opened my Christmas present to him: a moody black-and-white photograph of me standing on Lower Wacker Drive, my eyes full of soulful vulnerability, the collar of an old coat I'd bought at the Salvation Army turned up high against my cheek. I'd given copies of this same "Poor Boy" photo to my mother and father but they'd each reacted with puzzling silence, putting it aside as though they were ashamed of it. By grasping so quickly what I was after in Poor Boy—he'd even given it a name—my uncle redeemed it in my mind. For I'd been tremendously pleased with the look of it (it would make a great album cover for my first record, I thought), and no small part of its appeal was that its muted tones showed very little trace of the embarrassing acne that had started spotting my face here and there.

Down in the Washington Street subway station Uncle Eddie drew my attention to a man in a leather jacket standing down the platform from us. "He looks so much like this boy I met in a bar here a year ago," my uncle said, and a only a minute later did I realize that the "boy" he was talking about was in fact a man in his twenties, a medical student. "This boy and I talked for hours and hours and by the time we left the bar we'd decided to spend the rest of our lives together. The only problem was which city we'd live in, his or mine. In the end, of course, nothing came of it. He didn't want to leave his school and I couldn't see myself leaving all my friends behind in New York."

I asked how his friend the candy-atarian was doing and a little smile came to my uncle's thin lips as he told me how he'd gotten him a job sweeping the floors of a magazine and how the candy-atarian had immediately taken to entertaining everyone by doing the cancan as he pushed his broom along. Now he'd risen to office manager; by next month he'd no doubt be running the magazine. As we settled into our padded brown vinyl El seat, I asked my uncle about what had been so mysterious to me: why that other friend of his, the one who'd gone to the Cloisters with us, had said it was the best day of his life.

"Well, I did promise him I wouldn't say anything but then you have every right to ask. You see, he's what we call a 'chicken hawk'—someone who likes young boys, that is, or 'chicken.' But it's not like he'd ever think of imposing himself on a boy—he's actually very shy and reserved. For him it's enough just to be *around* a beautiful boy like your friend, Donny, who has those beautiful, strange pale eyes and that wonderful olive skin."

When Donny and I came back from New York, I remember I was still so bedazzled by my uncle and his friends that I found myself fantasizing that the Free School girl I had a secret crush on was told I was gay. And in my fantasy this news made her feel terribly impressed with me—made her love me, even. Because in the logic of my daydream to be gay was simply to be invested with that aura, that New Yorker aura, that Uncle Eddie and his friends all possessed. My uncle's chicken hawk story, however, had put being gay in a much more disturbing light. It wasn't the pederasty that bothered me. No, what hit too close to home was just that looks seemed to be so all-important. For though I'd heard people say that Donny, with his lithe body and fine, dark-brown hair extending down to the small of his back, was prettier than his sisters, I never would have thought of this as being the defining thing about him.

My uncle asked if I still saw a lot of Donny and I said I'd just stayed up half the night with him. It was Donny who'd taken the "Poor Boy" picture of me and when I decided at the last minute to make it my Christmas present to everyone, Donny spent hours in the eerie red safelight of his darkroom pulling large dripping prints of the photo out of the developing tray and then mounting them all for me. By the time he'd finished, it was going on four A.M. Christmas morning. Outside, a heavy wet snow had been falling for hours and I carried my Poor Boys home on my bike through the deserted streets, the only sound the sizzling of my tires cutting down through the snow to the gleaming asphalt underneath. It was a truly white night. The sky itself was white, and the air so deathly still that every little branch and twig had collected a load of sparkling snow two or three times its size. It seemed all at once weird, sad, and exciting to have missed spending Christmas Eve with my family and to be coming home only now with everyone asleep.

Now another special night was unfolding as I walked with my uncle along these same snowy Evanston streets. We'd gotten off the train at the dim little Noyes Street station, the only passengers left on the one-car Evanston El. But our house still lay a good couple miles away and it was weird to be walking with Uncle Eddie at my side, since every other adult I knew drove a car and wouldn't dream of hiking like this through the night and snow. I pointed out, when we came to it, the darkened Methodist church to which the Free School had relocated and my uncle surprised me by suggesting I write up my whole experience at the school. He said I could sell it to a magazine—perhaps to his magazine, *Horizon*, where he was a senior editor—and get maybe two thousand dollars for it. Beneath the rush of excitement I felt, however, lay the uneasy thought that my uncle didn't really know me or the Free School. I'd heard him breezily summing up the Free School to his friends in New York as "this place where the kids all voted out math," when the truth was that we'd never had math in the first place. I wondered if he could have any idea how little writing I'd done as a Free School student, how I lacked a desk at school and at home and how the only times I'd even put pen to paper lately were to scribble down song lyrics on scraps of paper at my feet in the attic as I strummed my guitar.

He said he'd heard from my mother that I was thinking of leaving the Free School and I told him I was leaning toward enrolling at Evanston High. "Have you ever considered going off to prep school?" he asked, stopping to light up one of his Kent cigarettes. In the flare of the lighter, his familiar deep-set eyes had a hooded, shadowed something to them that reminded me of a raccoon. "There's this wonderful school in Michigan called Interlochen that's completely devoted to the arts," he said. "It's the kind of place I wish I'd gone to."

Yet as with his writing-up-the-Free-School idea, I felt he was thinking too big for me. I couldn't imagine my mother and father ever agreeing to lay out the cash for such a fancy private school. As if reading my mind, my uncle said, "I suppose money might be a problem, but maybe I could help out. Life is so short, really, that we should only do what we really want to. And so, I don't know, if you found yourself wanting to come to New York, even—wanting to come live with me, I mean—well, I suppose I could get a bigger apartment and we could look around for a school for you there." Such an avalanche of generosity was hard to digest. I wanted to say something, to say thank you, but I didn't think I could say it without painfully embarrassing both of us.

By the time Uncle Eddie and I walked in the front door, my brother and sister had gone to bed and my mother was in a foul mood. She said she'd been waiting so long for us to show up that she'd been about to get in the car and go look for us. This struck me as a strange thing to say, but then I was used to her moodiness and sudden assertions of authority. She was capable of bursting in the door after having been absent for thirty-six hours and yelling at us kids about the house being a wreck. Or erupting at me about the garbage I was eternally saying I'd take out later. Sometimes I'd erupt right back at her and for a minute or two the house would rumble from this indoor thunderstorm. We'd hurl the most terrible words at each other.

Unbeknownst to me, my mother had told Uncle Eddie that she'd come to feel afraid of me during these arguments. The force of my will struck her as every bit as strong as her own, yet I now stood several inches taller than she. Of course, had anyone bothered to ask I could have said that my mother sometimes scared me. She was the one who'd grab a broomstick and brandish it at me. And she was the one who, when I couldn't take any more and went running out of the house, would yell after me, "Goddamnit, I'm calling the cops this time, I mean it!" It would never occur to me to wonder what I was guilty of. My heart pounding, I'd run out into the alley and go into hiding, listening for the sound of police sirens. The police never came, of course, and half an hour later the air would have cleared so completely that Mom and I could no longer remember the terrible things we'd said.

Now this Christmas night my mother and I were soon yelling at each other again about something or other right in front of Uncle Eddie. And when I went running out of the house, my uncle followed after me. He caught up with me in the alley and I remember thinking his sympathy for me seemed excessive. It made me feel guilty, awkward. Because as much as I burned with indignation about being misunderstood by my mother, I still didn't feel I deserved to have my side of things taken quite so seriously and dignified in this way. Later, from my bed up in the attic, the raised voices of my mother and uncle could be heard getting more and more heated downstairs.

The following evening I came along when my mother drove Uncle Eddie to the airport. From the backseat I heard my uncle tell my mother, "Keith and I have been talking about his coming to live with me in New York. Considering that he's already decided to leave the Free School, I just thought he might do better to get out of Evanston entirely and—"

"*What?*" my mother spit out, flabbergasted. "My son is *not* going to New York." No matter how Uncle Eddie and I tried to sweet-talk her, she was adamant that I was not going anywhere.

At the airport Uncle Eddie got out of the car without a good-bye, and the whole ride home with Mom I didn't say a word.

From New York, Eddie sent my mother a short letter:

Dear Marg,

I don't like the idea of our fighting. I was relieved to talk to Keith the next morning after our ugly exchange and to discover that everything is patched up between you two.

As for our own fight, I hope we can forget it and resume our old friendship. The two nasty fights we've had recently (our only fights since we've become adults, as best I recall) have both involved Keith; I think it's just that our feelings run very high when his future is uncertain. Perhaps we should resolve not to discuss him? Or, if some communication about him is necessary for practical reasons, perhaps we should commit it to the calmer medium of writing?

These disputes are really very upsetting to me. Yesterday I lost my Horizon job, which only added to my feelings of insecurity. To lose your friendship as well (in a family already so fragmented) would seem ghastly and unnecessary.

Love,
Ed

Years later my mother would tell me it had infuriated her that Eddie had not thought to consult her first (she was the mother, after all!) about bringing me to New York. Instead, he'd "gone and cooked this whole thing up behind my back so that I wound up looking like the bad guy." And yet for all this she said that even if Eddie had consulted her first, she still would have nixed the idea because at that time she didn't think it would be good for me to live with "a young gay man who was going out to gay bars every night and picking up men."

THE HORRORS TO COME

An air of mystery surrounds the key event in our family—my father's assuming custody of us three kids. Part of the mystery is just due to my own amnesia. The final months with Mom are such a crazy blur that I've blocked out what must have been the big turning point: the night I rode my bike all the way to Dad's apartment deep in the neighboring suburb of Skokie. It's my sister who remembers that Mom and I got into a "terrible argument" that night. Apparently I said something that made my mother so "hysterical" that she picked up my bowl of tomato soup and threw it at me. When it missed, the soup splattering against the wall, I went running out of the house and rode off to see Dad. I returned hours later, my sister says, telling her we might be going to live with our father.

My mother remembers things differently. She says I was so mad at her for vetoing Uncle Eddie's plan of bringing me to New York that I called up my father one night and told him she was gay. This was the one thing she'd made us kids swear we'd never tell him and by spilling the beans, she says, I provided my father with just the ammunition he'd been looking for. For my mother is convinced that Dad had been itching for the chance to steal us kids away from her. It would be his payback for all the hard times she'd put him through—the drinking, the breakdowns, the divorce he never wanted.

When Dad did take us away that spring of 1974, my mother claims he did so by threatening to expose her homosexuality in court if she dared to contest things. My father, however, denies all this. In his version, in fact, my mother, far from needing to be cowed with threats, *welcomed* his taking us off her hands, telling him she felt "incapable of being a parent" at that time.

However things actually happened, I have no doubt my father felt deeply bitter toward my mother. He once told me that she'd ruined his life. Divorce, let alone lesbianism, had no part in the "life plan" he'd carefully laid out for himself in 1958. And it particularly galled him that on top of everything else he'd had to cede our house on Pioneer Road to Mom, all those mortgage payments he'd worked so hard for down the drain.

My mother might have ruined his life but my father wasted no time in getting married again. At the end of 1971, the year of his and Mom's April Fool's Day divorce, he married a twenty-three-year-old woman he'd started dating after bumping into her at a record store where they'd each gone to buy the same album, Carole King's *Tapestry*, because they both felt a strong identification with the album's hit single, "It's Too Late." With her frizzy brass-brown hair, our new stepmother looked a bit like Carole King, though the look in her eyes was more ordinary and blunt.

One of the things about my father's version of events that's never added up for me, though, is those weird enticements he offered me. For if, as Dad has it, my sister and I practically begged him and our stepmother to let us come live with them because our life with Mom had gotten "really bad," then why did Dad feel he had to promise me a huge weekly allowance and even access to a well-stocked liquor cabinet to get me to agree to move in with them? It was this tempting bait he dangled in front of me that goes a long way toward answering the riddle of how I ever could have walked into something so disastrously ill-suited to me.

Yet the day we moved into the house Dad had rented was very odd and not at all a token of what was to come: my father, stepmother, and I got stoned together. Our new house, a two-story hodgepodge of dark brick and mock Tudor, stood just five blocks away from Mom and our old house on Pioneer Road. As we sat around in our new backyard, my father, his nose, cheeks, and big bald spot ruddy with summer sun, lit up a joint filled with some Jamaican Gold a friend had given him. I remember thinking to myself that I'd misjudged my father and stepmother: they had apparently been living a much hipper life than I'd ever suspected, a life that my father's full black beard and the rainbow patch my stepmother had sewn onto the back pocket of his blue jeans only hinted at. But then my head began to reel from the powerful marijuana. I felt higher than I'd ever been—too high. Like a seasick sailor I stumbled off to my new room down in the basement and fell heavily into bed. For hours I felt too dizzy and weak to do anything but lie there flat on my back, riding out my bad trip as my mind's eye tirelessly showed me a kaleidoscope of shapes and colors. When it was all over I swore off ever getting high again.

This strange start to life with Dad seemed all the stranger in coming days as I began to get the feeling of a trap snapping shut all around me. The big allowance he'd promised never materialized. The liquor cabinet was locked up. And he imposed a ten o'clock curfew and a ten-thirty bedtime on me—not an easy pill to swallow for a boy used to going off on his own for days and nights at a time (just a week before moving in with Dad, in fact,

I'd taken a three-day hitchhiking trip through Iowa and Wisconsin with my friend Donny). But my father never said a word about misrepresenting what life with him would be like. Nor did he seem to be making the slightest effort to understand what a difficult transition this all must be for someone like me. He was completely consumed with my stepmother. I hadn't realized to what extent she ruled his heart. In what would become a regular event, my father went around the house putting up signs with my stepmother's name on it that exclaimed, "You're Something Special!" and "We Love You!" He declared it her "appreciation day" and expected us to show her even more deference than usual. When my sister and I got into little disputes with her and went to Dad for mediation, he'd invariably side with our stepmother. If we pointed out his gross favoritism to him, he'd come right out and tell us, "Well, I'm sorry but my wife has to come first and you kids second." My mother, for all her eccentricities, had at least treated my brother, sister, and me as though we were interesting, important personalities. But now that we were under my father and stepmother's thumb, the feeling was more like we were orphans sent to live with an old farm couple who didn't take any truck from children.

Dumb me. You'd think I would have grasped from the time I first met her that my stepmother was a real handful. There'd been a terrible Sunday when I was twelve that she got right in my face and screamed at me till I cried—all because I'd run as hard as I could in the softball game we were playing and come sliding into home plate in a cloud of dust. "Goddamnit, don't be so fucking competitive!" she'd screamed, something that didn't make any sense to me because I'd just come out of Little League where, with Dad often shouting encouragement from the third base coach's box, I'd been urged to play the game at full throttle. Almost as shocking as my stepmother's fury was how Dad just stood there, limply, while she was lighting into me. Somehow I'd failed to see that my father had been taken over like a tree by creeper vine.

*   *   *

Our family cats, Rocky and O.J., didn't like our new house and within days had found their way back to Mom and the old house. After a couple weeks, I was ready to follow them home. My brother and sister, though, seemed resigned to sticking it out with my father and stepmother. Unlike me, they'd never left the structured world of the public schools and perhaps they even felt that, on balance, they'd gained more than they'd lost through this parental changing of the guard. Or maybe it was just that they were both far less willful and inclined to challenge things than I. In any event, one night I called up my mother and told her, "I want to come back with you—it's horrible here." But my mother said it couldn't be done. It was too late.

The next day a tremendous wave of nostalgia came over me at the sight of the three pine trees standing, as always, in front of our old house, the pine on the left side bluer and older-looking than the other two. Though I could see my mother was not at home because her car wasn't parked out front, I entered the glassed-in front porch. The giant, thickly ridged pinecones Mom had placed in a wicker basket years ago still lay there in a heap by the front door. But the living room window, through which I'd slipped into the house so many nights when I'd forgotten my key in my Free School days, was now locked tight. Suddenly feeling determined to get in, I ended up wriggling through a small window at the side of the house. A couple days later I slipped into Mom's house again through this same window but this time the doorbell rang and it was the police. Apparently the retired lady across the street, Mrs. Herr, had seen me climbing in the first time and alerted Mom. My mother had then instructed Mrs. Herr to call the cops if she saw me do it again.

As cold and hard as my mother's voice had sounded on the phone when she told me I couldn't come back because it was too late, I hadn't understood what a cauldron of emotions our move to Dad's had left seething within her. She felt angry, hurt, and, more than anything, terribly betrayed by us all.

The cops didn't exactly arrest me in Mom's house but they did take me down to the station, where I was held until my father came to pick me up. On the ride home, Dad acted totally exasperated by what I'd done. He bawled me out and then we rode along in charged silence. Hot tears were rolling down my cheeks and when we pulled up at a stop sign I had a sudden impulse to jump out of the car. But then I remembered there was no place left to run to.

For the crime of breaking and entering our old house I was assigned a probation officer I had to see once a month. By October I was also seeing the guidance counselor at Evanston High because of my chronic class-cutting. Many a morning I'd make a show of heading off for school, saying good-bye to Dad at the breakfast table and going out the door, only to sneak around to the far side of the house and slide myself in headfirst through my basement bedroom window. After a few more hours' sleep, I'd spend the rest of the day hanging out with my best friend, Bryan. He was not exactly the most likely high-school dropout. With his noble, grave good looks (he had very pale skin and dark curly hair) and his eyebrows arched in quiet attentiveness, Bryan still looked like the mild, dutiful boy who until the past year had attended the local seven A.M. Catholic mass each Sunday by himself, the only boy in a sea of little old ladies. But in the wake of his parents' recent divorce, Bryan decided one dawn, after a night of philosophical pacing, to drop out of school— even though he'd just received an A in the advanced algebra course he'd taken for extra credit at summer school.

I'd gotten to know Bryan while helping a bunch of neighborhood kids build a small wooden clubhouse in the messy backyard of David Hill, the boy who'd first suspected my mother and her AA group were all gay. We called our funky clubhouse "the fort" and Bryan and I would hang out in it when our bigger, better clubhouse—Bryan's house—wasn't available. Yet most of the time his house was ideally free of parental intrusions. Like my own mother after her divorce, Bryan's mom had gone out and gotten herself a job as well as a lover at whose Chicago apartment she often spent the night. And so Bryan and I would sit around in his living room, happily diddling away the hours drinking cups of instant coffee, smoking Marlboros, and playing music—either records on the stereo or our own music on guitars. Our lives revolved around music but I have Bryan to thank for bringing me into contact with Jean-Paul Sartre's *Nausea*, a book whose title made me laugh with approval. Soon I'd formed a whole notion of *Nausea* that had very little to do with the actual text, which I found slow going and a bit boring in its details. No, what I got from *Nausea* was an attitude toward life— my own attitude, really, but authenticated now by this world-famous novel—an attitude that let me dismiss Dad and everything else weighing me down as meaningless, absurd. It was this attitude, this almost jaunty hatred of our suburban reality, that made me and Bryan keep the drab gold curtains in his living room pulled shut against what we called, in a favorite phrase from *Nausea*, "the hideous light of day."

Nausea was in my lap the Sunday afternoon when everything erupted so nastily. Like a lot of family fights, what set this one off was totally petty and incidental. The anger that had been rising to dangerous levels between me and my father and stepmother was looking for the tiniest spark to set itself ablaze, and on this day it was my shoes. I happened to be reading stretched out on the bright-orange living room couch with my shoes on when Dad, who'd been vacuuming in the back of the house, came noisily into the living room, dragging the vacuum cleaner. Over the roar of the machine he shouted at me to take my shoes off the couch. Something in his voice, an irritating note of challenge, made me set my jaw and ask him, "Why?"

This made my father go bananas: "Because it's my goddamn house and you're going to goddamn do what I *tell* you to do, goddamnit!" He reached down as though to yank my legs off the couch but I shook him off furiously and leaped to my feet, pushing off against his chest as I backed up to get my balance, get some space. The room was spinning and howling. The vacuum cleaner, knocked over on its side but still roaring, now found itself in the middle of things as my father and I circled each other warily, our arms up and poised like boxers looking for an opening. I'd never fought with Dad physically before, never fought for real with anybody. But Bryan had just been showing me how you tucked your thumb inside your fist and threw a punch directly outward from your chest. Though my father was a good thirty pounds heavier than I, I felt so flooded with anger, so goaded by *his* anger, that I was ready to see if I could take him. But then came the oddest moment: my father was standing there before me and yet a violent force, a weight, was being applied to my back and shoulders. How, I wondered, could he be both in front of and behind me?

The riddle was solved when my father rushed over and helped my stepmother wrestle me to the floor and pin me there. She must have come running when she heard me and Dad arguing and then jumped me from behind like a wild Apache. With my father sitting on my stomach and holding down my arms, my stepmother squatted beside my head, her face red and contorted as she pulled out whole hanks of my hair by the roots and kept screaming down at me, "Had enough? Huh? Had enough yet?"

When they finally let me go I was trembling with shock and exhaustion and humiliation and rage. I staggered down to my basement room and saw that my face, which felt sticky and itched like crazy from all the pulled-out hair plastered to my cheeks and eyes, was a mess of snot and tears.

I'd always kind of hated the color orange but now I really couldn't stand it. During my long talk with Uncle Eddie Christmas night he'd happened to mention the way we can project our strongest emotions onto the innocent objects around us, and that's what I was doing now with all the orange stuff in the house. The rage that made me want to pound my father and stepmother's bedroom door and yell *Fuck you!* at them had gotten all mixed up with how much I hated their horrible orange couch and their stupid orange plastic dinner plates that we had to eat off of every night. Yet unbearable as life was getting for me with Dad, it never crossed my mind to write or call up Uncle Eddie. He seemed more remote than ever—I guess because I wasn't seeing much of my mother these days. She'd sold our old house on Pioneer Road and moved into a lakeside apartment down in the city with Phyllis. But part of it too was my sense that Uncle Eddie was a creature of the moment, someone who could be moved to heights of sympathy and generosity when you were in his presence but who, when you were "offstage" in his life, could completely forget that you existed. The whole fantasy of going off to live with him now seemed as far-fetched as my ever writing a two-thousand-dollar article about the Free School. It had all vanished with the special mood of that winter night.

Quite seriously, I began to think about running off to live in a small cave or burrow that I would dig out in some secret, overgrown place along the bank of the sanitary canal. As a boy my favorite book had been *My Side of the Mountain*. It told the story of this very handy kid who manages to live for a year in a hollow tree in the woods. Though I myself knew nothing about living in the wild—how to make a fire, which berries to eat—I did know I was prepared to go to extremes to get free from my dad. And I did have one very practical thought: since we were into October now I'd better start digging before the ground hardened with frost.

But then I decided to run away to New Orleans. I got the idea from "City of New Orleans," one of Bryan's and my favorite songs, and when I mentioned the scheme to Bryan he unexpectedly said he wanted to join me. Bryan had some money of his own but I needed to get hold of about seventy dollars—the fare for a one-way train ticket. He and I would get jobs as soon as we hit New Orleans, I decided. I saw us living in an apartment empty of furniture, reading the newspaper down on the hardwood floor each morning before going off to our jobs in a gloomy warehouse. For I realized I had to be realistic; I couldn't expect to make my living right away as a performer in the French Quarter. I'd have to pay my dues.

After contemplating robbing an old lady of her purse on the street, I decided to steal the money from my father. He kept his wallet in his top dresser drawer, something I knew about because when my sister and I made regular raids on the deep bowl of loose change atop his dresser, we'd also been unable to resist snooping through all the dresser drawers, discovering among other things that my father and stepmother each kept diaries full of titillating details about their marital problems.

Stealing the money went like a dream. Though Dad's wallet contained well over a hundred dollars, I made it a point of honor to take no more than the seventy I needed. As I headed downstairs with the bills burning in my pocket, I passed my father on the stairs and marveled at how calmly I was able to look him in the eye and make some offhand remark.

My suitcase and guitar were waiting down in my basement room. My plan called for me to heave them and myself up and out my little side window so that I could make my getaway from the house without being seen. But when I picked up the suitcase it was so heavy that I realized it would be too much to lug my guitar along as well. The guitar would have to be left behind.

Very fittingly, the song that inspired our flight is actually not about the city of New Orleans but the City of New Orleans, the train that makes a daily nine-hundred-mile run from Chicago down to the Bayou. Fitting, because it turned out Bryan and I spent far more time aboard the train than we did in New Orleans. We arrived at noon the next day feeling groggy and disoriented in the hot, steamy air. After consulting the help-wanted ads but not finding anything, we struggled down to a waterfront esplanade with our heavy suitcases to plot our next move. A local man stopped to chat with us, explaining that the wide expanse of water, full of ships and birds, we'd taken for the Gulf of Mexico was in fact the Mississippi River delta. When we asked him about prospects for work, he just laughed and said, "How do you kids expect to find work when this town don't have enough jobs for adults?" He suggested we try nearby Baton Rouge instead.

With the last of our money we took a Greyhound bus to Baton Rouge, but at the bus station there I went to the men's room and the sight of my face in the mirror was so appalling, so dispiriting, that all the air went out of my hopes for everything. It was hard to believe that the acne sprouting up all over my face lately could have gotten so much worse in just the past twenty-four hours. I told Bryan I didn't feel like bothering with looking for jobs in Baton Rouge, that I wanted to start hitchhiking back to Chicago immediately. Though I offered no explanation, the ever-agreeable Bryan accepted this huge change of plan. Just what Bryan himself thought about things could be difficult to know, so prone was he to becoming infused with the wishes of those around him. He was sympathetic in the original meaning of the word: to feel another's feelings.

For more than an hour we stood watching cars whiz past our outstretched thumbs. Finally a pickup truck stopped. Though the driver told us he wasn't going far, we hopped in the open back of his truck and after a windy ride on the expressway were dropped off in the industrial outskirts of town. Night was falling. We started walking along the shoulder of a two-lane road that I could see reached a T up ahead where a long factory with belching smokestacks blocked the way. Suddenly a glass bottle thrown from a passing car shattered at our feet. Then another bottle came flying. It dawned on me that all the faces in the cars going past were black. I started to panic and when I found a pay phone I called the police.

When a squad car pulled up, I admitted straight out that we were runaways from Chicago. The cop seemed amused that two young Yanks had "gone a-stumblin' into darkie town." He took us to a home for delinquent boys where we were made to strip, shower, and raise our arms so that we could be sprayed for lice. Because we'd had the bad timing to turn ourselves in on a Friday night, we were forced to spend the weekend each locked up in a solitary cell in our underwear—the juvenile judge wouldn't be back on the bench till Monday morning. Going through our suitcases, a young staff member happened upon *Nausea* and exclaimed, "Well, lookee here, they're readin' Sartre," which he pronounced so that it rhymed with *farter*.

On Monday the judge decreed that Bryan and I be put on a Greyhound bus back to Chicago. Our parents were contacted and asked to wire the bus fare. My father, however, was apparently so angry that he refused to send any money, saying I should be left to straggle the nine hundred miles home as best I could. Only when Bryan's mother called Dad up to plead with him did he grudgingly give in. Bryan's mother said my stepmother, who'd also gotten on the line, sounded particularly "mean."

In the short time Bryan and I had been away it seemed like all the leaves in Evanston had come falling down. The sight of so many desolate trees filled me with a bleak November feeling: the world had darkened and grown more serious. My father had a nasty surprise of his own waiting for me—he'd impounded my most precious possession, the acoustic guitar I'd bought with money earned cleaning the Free School gutters. Dad said my guitar would stay locked up in a janitor's closet at his elementary school till I'd paid him back the hundred-some dollars I now owed him. With cruel accuracy my friends and I started referring to my father as "the Crapper" among ourselves because Dad's face these days often wore a wincing grimace that reminded us of someone straining to take a difficult crap.

Soon my father's house had become a house of pain for me in another, quite literal way: I'd started torturing my face each day with an acne "treatment" I'd devised. My grandmother Delilah had taken me aside one day and said that at her clinic for the mentally retarded the teenagers afflicted with acne had gotten great results from "soaping up a hand towel and scrubbing their face just as hard as they could." My mother, meanwhile, had given me several boxes of something called Retin A, which she used on her own face whenever it broke out with a blackhead or two. I decided to combine the two treatments and the first time I swabbed the alcohol-based Retin A onto my face after having scrubbed it into a raw, bloody, oozing mess with a hand towel, tears leapt to my eyes from the hotly stinging pain. The pain was so unbelievable that I thought it must be doing some good. Even after a friend confided to me, "I think your face has turned into one hard, giant pimple," I clung to the idea that my face had to get worse before it got better. If it didn't get better, it could only be because acne as bad as mine was unique, untreatable.

One day not long after Christmas my father told me he'd made an appointment for me, him, and my stepmother with a family therapist. I didn't particularly welcome the idea but I didn't really mind it so much either. A few years back, during one of my parents' separations, Dad and I had gone to see a family therapist a couple times and I'd noticed how much better I performed in these settings than he did. The therapist always seemed to end up sympathizing with my side of things because at some point I'd be sure to start crying, which would get the therapist dabbing at his eyes and smiling at me tenderly.

This latest family therapist, Dr. Johnson, turned out to be a psychiatrist with an office in nearby Evanston Hospital. His little office was up on the fifth floor, just across from the elevator bank, and coming out of the elevator I happened to look to my left for a split second and caught a glimpse of what appeared to be the entrance to a psychiatric ward. But I forgot all about this as young, very reasonable-seeming Dr. Johnson shook my hand and ushered us into the now-familiar world of the one-hour therapy session. I felt confident I would get a fair hearing and, judging from the kindly look the doctor was giving me, a whole lot of sympathy too.

A few minutes into therapy, however, I heard the first gentle mention of my "staying here"—staying here on the fifth floor in the psychiatric ward! Because I was still under the impression that nothing had been decided for sure, that Dr. Johnson was a judge who could be appealed to, I tried to make my case for staying free, telling the doctor with mounting alarm that I'd be willing, very willing, to be an outpatient, just not an inpatient, please. I could even see him several times a week if he wanted. But when it became obvious that all argument was futile I stood up and left the office. As I waited, trembling, for the elevator to come, Dad and Dr. Johnson came out and tried to sweet-talk me into not leaving. But no one laid a hand on me as I got onto the elevator alone. Thinking on my feet, I decided not to risk going down to the lobby, and got off instead on the second floor (a good idea, I found out later, since Dr. Johnson had immediately telephoned security and told them to intercept me in the lobby).

Next to the elevator bank I found a door opening onto a stairway. I scrambled down a flight and a half of stairs, past the lobby level, stopping on a landing halfway down to the basement. Like a hunted animal, I wanted to be poised to flee in either direction. But the stairwell remained eerily empty and silent. Five minutes, ten minutes went by. It was hard to stand still with my mind racing and heart pounding: How many people were looking for me? Was this really happening? Was this my *life* now?

Finally, weary of the suspense of waiting, I decided to risk making a getaway. I crept down the last half-flight of stairs, pulled the door open, and found myself in the bowels of the hospital. The noisy shuddering of heavy machinery and the shouts of maintenance men filled the air. Under a low ceiling of exposed wiring, I threaded my way past big carts of dirty laundry and cases of Pepsi stacked high on wooden skids. Nobody paid any attention to me as I slipped out an open door into the winter dusk.

I was at the service entrance on the back side of the hospital, where deliveries are made and trash hauled away. Orienting myself, I realized that the dark expanse a hundred yards dead ahead was the Evanston Community Golf Course. The sky above me was purpling with night, a big star already shining brightly, as I jogged across the snow-covered fairway, heading for the line of trees on the far side where the sky was graduating from pale blue to green to sooty orange. Behind that line of trees, I knew, lay my old friend the sanitary canal—the perfect escape route! I wanted to get down by the water, out of sight, and the steep, wooded bank had me stumbling over roots and skidding on wet leaves beneath the snow. Thickets raked my hands and coat, and low-hanging branches had to be pushed through like turnstiles. But down by the water's edge it was much easier going. I supposed if need be I could even cross over the canal whose murky waters were now iced over and covered with snow.

The sky had very quickly grown completely dark. A branch snapped sharply underfoot just as I noticed some lights flashing on the bridge up ahead. For an instant I panicked: could the police have set up a roadblock for me? Then I realized the flashing lights were *yellow*. It was only a utility truck parked up there and some innocent bridge repair work going on.

Picking my way carefully through the dark, I followed the canal south toward my old neighborhood and the network of back alleys I was so familiar with. Within half an hour I was at Bryan's house and rapping at his back door. Instantly sympathetic as always, Bryan took me up to his attic bedroom, where we decided I would live as a stowaway in the long crawl space underneath the slanting roof. Twice a day or more he would bring up secret meals to me on a tray. The almost vegetable patience such holing up would require of me, not to speak of the devotion demanded of Bryan, never entered our minds. In fact, just a few minutes later he and I had already gotten so restless that we left the house and crossed the street to the little wooden "fort" in David Hill's junky backyard. While I waited alone in the fort, Bryan ran around the neighborhood rounding up our friends, telling them about the exciting predicament I was in. Soon there were seven of us huddled together in the fort, singing songs and stamping our feet against the cold on the dirty rug laid on top of the hard earth.

It was becoming such a bitterly cold January night that David Hill said we should go warm up in his basement bedroom for a while. So we all trooped into his house and went down there and just as I was getting comfortable enough to forget I was on the run (David was a huge Kurt Vonnegut fan and he'd started filling us in on the high jinks to be found in Vonnegut's newest masterpiece, *Breakfast of Champions*), the "Gestapo," as we ever after would call them, suddenly showed up. Down the steep wood basement steps came the clomping of heavy black boots. It was two policeman, one behind the other. Like all cops, they seemed too big for the indoors with their squawking walkie-talkies and holstered guns.

"All right, the jig is up. Which one of you is Keith Fleming?"

Bryan stepped forward heroically and said, "I am."

They marched Bryan up the steps but ran into David Hill's mother up in the kitchen who informed them that they hadn't nabbed Keith Fleming (my father had apparently called Mrs. Hill and all the other parents of my friends, telling them to phone the police the minute they saw me). Furious, the cops stormed back downstairs and dragged me off in handcuffs.

With everything under control in the squad car, though, the cops became more friendly. It seemed to amuse them to have to be taking some kid to the psycho ward. "Whuhd-juh do—pull some crazy stunt?" one of them said to me with a laugh. "Well, just take it easy in there and you'll be out in a couple weeks." By the time we reached the fifth floor I'd so accepted the situation that I actually took pride in making such a sensational entrance onto the ward. Heads turned and meek eyes widened with awe at the sight of me being escorted to the nurses' station like a dangerous criminal, hands still behind my back in the cuffs, flanked by big cops. For a minute there—from across the room at least—I thought I must have been looking pretty cool.

Later that night Bryan, David Hill, and several other neighborhood kids all showed up en masse at Evanston Hospital and tried to see me. They were turned away, but their show of support so impressed the psycho ward staff that, according to my mother, the nurses immediately suspected it must be my father and not I who had the real problems. How bad could a boy be with so many loyal friends?

But though my friends now regarded me as a "political prisoner," Evanston Hospital was far from being a prison. After a couple days on the locked side of the ward, where only the real crazies stayed, I was deemed fit for the larger, unlocked side when I gave my solemn promise not to try to run away again. And why would I? Life in many ways was better in the bughouse than at Dad's house. My new room was a lot like a room at a Holiday Inn, lacking only the TV. Each morning maids came in to straighten out the mess I'd made, making up the bed, emptying ashtrays, cleaning up the bathroom. I no longer had school to worry about and was free to spend hours every day playing my guitar, which my father had returned to me as a sort of consolation prize, I guess. With my guitar back I was able to resume what had been the most important part of my life during the past year: performing three or four songs at the Sunday Night Open Stage of a local pizza parlor called the Spot.

The Spot's master of ceremonies was someone who'd taken me under his wing, thrilling me by saying I could "make a lot of money someday" as a performer—not because I was such a good singer or guitar player but "because the things you say are so funny, even though you always act like you don't want to be up there onstage. And the songs you write are getting better." At twenty-one this M.C. was just six years older than I. But with his deft stage patter, handlebar mustache, and lean, foxlike face he seemed infinitely older, a true adult. Now that I was in the bughouse, in fact, he and the elegant, pretty girlfriend who always accompanied him told me they'd been discussing the idea of adopting me and having me come live with them out in Morton Grove.

Late in the afternoon on Sundays my mother would show up at the psycho ward to sign me out on pass. After stopping by to pick up my brother and sister, we'd all go to the Spot for dinner, staying there all evening until I'd had my chance to sing. One night my father and stepmother turned up unexpectedly, taking a back table. For my final number I sang a song I'd just written that satirized my hospitalization. There was a line in the chorus that went something like "So why don't you come and reha-bil-lah-bilatate me?" By song's end my stepmother, who'd recently dyed her hair much blonder, was on her feet, shouting so loudly that it competed with my amplified voice coming out of several loudspeakers placed throughout the restaurant. "Yeah, that's right, you *should* be rehabilitated!" she yelled. "Rehabilitation is what you *need*!"

My father and stepmother had provided my psychiatrist, Dr. Johnson, with a bunch of evidence they'd secretly collected documenting my disturbed state of mind. I can't remember whether Dr. Johnson showed me or just told me about them, but there were several photographs of the unsavory state of my basement bedroom. More shocking, Dad and Stepmom had gone rifling through my personal notebooks and made photocopies of the sickest song lyrics they could find. I never bothered to explain to Dr. Johnson how lyrics I'd scribbled such as "I know you don't feel for me / But you are not really real to me" were often more influenced by the need to rhyme and find words that sounded good to sing than anything I wanted to confess. Or how simply strumming a D-minor chord could get me wanting to declare something dramatic and sad.

I never bothered explaining much to Dr. Johnson because he never seemed disturbed by anything about me. If anything, he was *too* approving, too ready to believe that deep down in me everything was fine. We never discussed my horrible acne, my worries about going through life without ever having a girlfriend, or my fantasies about leaving Evanston to live in a car that I would drive across pastures and forests. I was afraid to disappoint him and pucker his unmarked, good-natured face.

By March Dr. Johnson had completed his evaluation, pronouncing me fit to go home. But from what I could gather (I never heard anything from my father directly), Dad didn't want

me back home again. So Dr. Johnson suggested that I be sent
to a boarding school in the posh northern suburb of Lake Bluff.
For a week it looked like this was where I would be going, which
was okay by me, but then my father must have decided he was
unwilling to pay for such an expensive boarding school because
the new word from Dr. Johnson was that I would probably be
going home after all.

The morning I was released my father told me he wanted us
to go see another psychiatrist he'd been in contact with. Dad
promised that this time it really would be just a brief consulta-
tion. We were standing out in the Evanston Hospital parking
lot, I remember, under a deep blue sky. But what I can't remember is what on earth I could have been thinking as I climbed
into Dad's car, a maroon Torino. Did I really not smell another
trap? I mean, hadn't my father already tricked me twice, first to
get me to move in with him, then to get me into Evanston
Hospital? Could it have been that I just felt too weighed down—
a suitcase in one hand, a guitar case in the other—to make a
run for the canal bank again? Or had my experience with Dr.
Johnson made me confident that every other psychiatrist would
also find me to be fine? Or was being hospitalized again something I didn't even particularly object to anymore? After all, the
most memorable thing I'd ever heard about mental hospitals was
when Uncle Eddie told me about a good friend of his who'd
taken a delightful "tour of the local bughouses," finding at every
step of the way loads of interesting new people and plenty of
time for reading.

CHAPTER 4

DR. SCHWARZ
AND LAURA

My father drove us across the city to the western suburb of Berwyn, where we pulled up in front of a tired-looking hospital called McNeal Memorial. Once again we rode an elevator to the fifth floor but this time a nurse took us down a grim hallway, unlocking and ushering us through a thick metal door painted hospital beige with a little window of wired glass built into it. The nurse led me and Dad down another hall to the open doorway of a shadowy office in which a venetian blind was letting in only very thin stripes of bright sunlight onto the floor. Inside this office a man in his late forties sat slouched deep in a swivel chair, talking on the phone. His head lolled back with regal casualness. His salt-and-pepper hair stuck straight up in a kind of weird, longish crewcut.

"Dr. Schwarz?" the nurse said, announcing us.

He turned his head and a pair of exhausted-looking, half-closed greenish-brown eyes took us in. "Of course!" he exclaimed into his phone in a strangely merry falsetto, leaping forward in his chair and beckoning the nurse over to his desk where he handed her some papers. As the nurse gestured for my father to come over and sign something, Dr. Schwarz was breezily saying into his phone, "Yes, I think she'll be an excellent student again once she learns she can't shit on you whenever she feels like it. All right?"

Hanging up, Dr. Schwarz told my father, "Okay, Dad, you're not needed here anymore. We'll be in touch."

Now Dr. Schwarz and I were alone. In his funny high voice, he told me, "Come in, come in! Sit down. Your father has just signed over power of attorney to me. Do you have any idea what this means? Hmmm? I wonder if you do." He was flipping through some papers on his lap, a crooked smile growing on his lips. Then something he read made him chuckle and I heard the sound of spit being sucked on noisily through his teeth.

"So you're from Evanston, I see," he said, smacking on his spit. "You must know Colette Marchetti, then, yes? She fucked just about every guy at Evanston High who had some drugs to share, didn't she? And Haven Stack. Boy, he must have been a *very* good friend, I bet. Yes? He was the only really big-time dealer in town, wasn't he? Yes, yes. You know, it's amazing what bad boys and girls will do and how much we know about it." As I wondered whether to pipe up and say that I didn't know these well-known delinquents and in any event hadn't gotten high in more than six months, I saw there was no stopping Dr. Schwarz, no opening to say anything. It was amazing how full of saliva his mouth was as it worked on, strings of spittle occasionally stretching and snapping off just inside the corners of his mouth.

"Power of attorney, Keith, means that your custody has been turned over to me and that I can do whatever I want with you. Understand? So if you're not prepared to be a good boy—if you want to be an asshole and not cooperate with us here—well, then we'll just have to put you in the isolation room and tie you down in restraints until you're ready to be nice. Oh yes." Dr. Schwarz was nodding and smiling, fixing me with those lazy, hooded eyes. "And if you still want to be an asshole after that, we'll just say good-bye. I have an arrangement with a prison farm I know of." He'd risen to his feet—he was a surprisingly small, slight man. "Oh yes! A nice little prison farm down in Alabama where the black convicts just love to fuck white boys up the ass. So it's very simple, you see. You can make nice and we can be friends or you can go to Alabama. Questions?"

I'd never had insomnia before but beginning that long first night I always slept badly on the ward at McNeal. Every hour or so I'd hear the squeaking of rubber-soled shoes out in the hall and then the door would be flung open by one of the night nurses making the rounds, her flashlight searching out the sleeping faces of me and my roommate across the room. I'd always pretend to be asleep but that first night I got to feeling so bad that I finally went padding down the long linoleum hallway toward the nurses' station to ask for something to help me sleep. But the night nurses weren't in their glass-encased nurses' station. Like a quartet of grandmothers, somebody else's gruff grandmothers, they were sitting out in the dayroom, playing cards and smoking. "Hey, it's against the rules to leave your room at night," one of them told me.

"Oh, sorry, I just can't seem to fall asleep," I said. Sensing they neither knew nor cared who I was, I added, "It's my first night here."

"Well, maybe this one time we can let him sit there and drink some milk," she said to the others. "Better make it snappy, though, because it won't be long before Dr. Schwarz is here, if he's coming today."

Sure enough, back in my room, while the windows were still black with night, the overhead lights suddenly snapped on and

Dr. Schwarz came strolling in. "Hello, hello!" he called out in his merry falsetto. Addressing my roommate, he said, "So! What's new with you?"

My roommate was gamely pulling himself together, propping himself up on an elbow in his narrow bed and wiping the sleep out of his handsome, squinting face with the back of his other forearm. "Doc," he said, "I was talking to my parents on pass last weekend. We think I'm making such, uh, such great progress that maybe I'll be ready to go home pretty soon."

Dr. Schwarz had thrown himself into the little green armchair by the window and was lolling there, eyes closed. "That's not what I heard," Schwarz told him. "I heard you showed up at a big pot party in Highland Park Saturday night."

"Doc, I didn't get high, I swear."

"Ah yes, so they all say!" With a dismissive wave of the hand Schwarz cut the boy's protests off and turned his face to me, his green-brown eyes half-opening like a lazy lizard's. "And you, what do you have to say for yourself?"

My mind went blank. "Me? Oh, uh, nothing. Nothing, really."

"I see. Well, how about standing up? Stand up."

"You mean now?" Under the covers I was just in my underwear and a T-shirt.

"Yes, I'm supposed to give you a physical."

When I shyly stood before him, he just shrugged and, still slouched in the chair, said, "You're healthy! So tell me. Are you a virgin?"

"Me? Uh . . . no," I lied.

"He's a virgin," Schwarz said to my roommate, his face lighting up.

I was sure that my roommate, now sitting up and gathering his long shiny hair into a ponytail, had lost his virginity long ago. With his high cheekbones, hollow cheeks, taut, chiseled face, and slitted eyes, he looked like a dark blond Indian brave. His wiry body had a casual but coiled masculinity to it and though he couldn't have been more than sixteen, his deep voice already sounded scarred with cigarettes. When Dr. Schwarz had left us a minute later I asked my roommate about the Alabama prison farm and he said that Schwarz threatened all the boys with that (girls were threatened with a convent full of predatory lesbian nuns). But though this was "bullshit," everything else Schwarz said was "for real." Seizing temporary custody of you from your parents, having you tied down in the isolation room if you didn't "cooperate"—it was all part of his standard operating procedure. As was this dawn visit. Except for his first meeting with you, Schwarz never saw you in his office, preferring to make sudden appearances deep in the night because he believed that waking you up allowed him to confront you when your "defenses were down."

During my meeting with Schwarz in his office, he'd snickered at one point and dismissed the psych ward at Evanston Hospital as a "country club." Now that I was in McNeal I could see what he meant. The fifth floor at Evanston Hospital, with its deep carpeting, private rooms, and mellow reading lamps placed amidst the elegant sofas and armchairs of the spacious dayroom, allowed patients to coexist in separate, dignified private universes. Meals could be taken on a tray to one's room and eaten there in solitude. The staff hovered discreetly in the wings, like good waiters who know at a glance whether you need them or wish to be left alone. At Evanston I never even spoke to most of my fellow patients. I'd been one of just three teenagers on the ward, everyone else being grown-ups who'd suffered nervous breakdowns. Occasionally you'd see one of these adults quietly crying and murmuring on a telephone near the nurses' station, but the reigning calm of the ward would absorb even this, leaving the overall impression that these people were on a kind of sabbatical from the pressures of marriage and professional lives. There were no grueling, embarrassing group therapies. Evanston was not so much a country club as a sanitarium where everyone sat around as though nursing drinks by the fireside, plunged in healing contemplation. On that very gentle ward, where the EXIT sign glowed at the end of the shadowy hallway above the unlocked doors, I'd heard the guiding philosophy described as "Gestalt," which was defined for me as meaning "anything goes."

Far from being a "Gestalt" ward, McNeal was a "structured environment for adolescents." All two dozen of us teenage patients belonged to Dr. Schwarz. None of us kids heard voices in our heads or had experienced anything like a Sylvia Plath–type breakdown or suicide attempt—no, we patients were all guilty of nothing more dramatic than cutting classes, telling Dad "fuck you" once too often, running away, or having our marijuana stashes discovered. But Dr. Schwarz had a growing reputation throughout suburban Chicago as someone able to "get through to" uppity teens whom other, milder, measures had failed to change. Many of my fellow patients were, like me, from Chicago's North Shore suburbs, though I noticed these suburbs tended to be wealthier and farther up the shore—Glencoe, Winnetka, Highland Park. More than a few high-powered parents, I learned, hoped that the "Schwarz treatment" would not merely make their kid shape up but also help to power Peter or Pamela on to Harvard or Yale.

The Schwarz treatment took place on a ward that was locked, cramped, and crowded. "The unit," as everyone called the ward, was lit by harsh overhead fluorescent lights and we kids slept two to a room in spartan quarters outfitted with narrow beds that were actually couches with sheets on them. First thing every morning we'd lift up the hollow, wooden back of the couches and stow our pillows in the compartment there that also stored our clothes. Then we'd pull a rough green fitted coverlet over the sheets, which we laundered ourselves each Monday. The unit was divided into boys' and girls' sides that were mirror images of each other: an outer dormitory wing flanking a dingy dayroom of worn, dirty carpeting, beat-up sofas, and long banquet tables at which we sat on folding chairs to eat our meals. The two dayrooms adjoined each other, and though boys could wander into the girls' dayroom during free time, we weren't allowed to set foot in the girls' dormitory wing. The slightest "p.c."—

physical contact—between boys and girls, including handshakes and pats on the back, was also strictly forbidden.

As was masturbation (how this one was supposed to be enforced, though, I never knew; I continued jerking off as much as ever in the privacy of the bathroom). But the Schwarz treatment involved all sorts of other rules that, as in prisons, were disobeyed at the risk of being thrown in an isolation cell or having privileges stripped away. A new patient like me discovered that just about everything had been declared a "privilege": the right to go home on weekend pass, to make phone calls, even to receive mail. And before these privileges could be lost, they had to be earned. It took a good couple weeks to accumulate the necessary merit points for mail and phone privileges, even more time before a weekend pass home became a possibility. But unlike in prison one didn't earn these points just through being obedient and cooperative—oh, no. For the final touch to the totalitarian system Dr. Schwarz had put in place was the way we kids were pitted against one another. Schwarz believed that even on the strictest psycho ward patients settled into a comfortable mind-set of *us versus them*, of seeing themselves as united against doctor and staff. To prevent this, he divided and conquered us kids by making ratting on fellow patients a part of our "progress." Each evening veteran patients went around clutching clipboards, interrogating the newer patients about their long day spent in all kinds of aggressive group therapies, sniffing out and reporting on any hint of a "counterproductive attitude."

After two months on the unit I'd earned enough points to qualify for weekend passes home. There was never any doubt about which parent I would spend the weekend with—I hadn't heard a word from my father since he'd deposited me with Dr. Schwarz and signed me away. And so each Saturday morning my mother and Phyllis would come to collect me in Phyl's car, a green Pacer with those distinctive, rounded bubble windows. But what I remember best is Sunday nights riding under the bubble in the Pacer's backseat, the pink night sky of the city above me, terrible butterflies in my stomach as each mile brought me closer and closer to being back in Dr. Schwarz's gulag. At these times the song playing on the Pacer's powerful quadraphonic sound system always seemed to be the eerie "I'm Not in Love (Big Boys Don't Cry)," with its deep cello notes of doom and hypnotic banks of voices.

Almost as bad was first thing weekday mornings, standing at the wire-mesh windows in my room. The fifth-floor view was a commanding one that looked out miles into the distance, to the thick belt of treetops in Oak Park, the much wealthier suburb to the north. I remember gazing out on shimmering mornings early in May at the beautiful smoky mist on the horizon. I could feel the freshness of the new day just looking at it. It was the time of year the Japanese call "Golden Week," the kind of weather that had always set my body to humming with pleasure and filled my head with thoughts of running away somewhere. And yet in no part of my mind did I ever step back and say, It's wrong that I'm in here. My acne was erupting worse than ever now that I was continually anxious and fearful and it filled me with such self-hatred that I had little sense of outrage about being locked up; obviously, there was something deeply wrong with me. Anyway, what was the point of being free if I would still be stuck behind such a horrible-looking face? Anywhere I went I'd feel like a leper.

The strangest effect of the Schwarz treatment was that practically every kid ended up idolizing him a bit as well as fearing him. Part of it was that Schwarz's long absences from the unit made it easier to see him as a mythic figure who towered over our lives. In the dayroom we patients liked to sit around discussing every aspect of him: the distinctive singsong voice and its love of rising up into falsetto on certain words he'd draw out: *Soooo!* But of *cooourse!* The stiff hair sticking up like porcupine quills. The self-satisfied mouth always munching on its abundant spit. The strange glee. The sharp words so at odds with the devil-may-care shrugs and distracted air. And, of course, the dawn visits that were more like visitations, since they began with a stab of light in our sleeping eyes and ended just a minute or two later. Sometimes Schwarz would be so tired when he came in the room that he'd plop himself down in the chair, murmur a favorite proclamation ("Sex is not necessary for teenagers! The only reason girls ever put out is because they really just want a hug and some attention"), and then, the lids of his hooded green-brown eyes getting heavier and heavier, he'd seem to nod off for a minute before rousing himself and heading off to wake up the kids in the next room. This heroic exhaustion was a big part of his image. He told us he was lucky to get two hours sleep a night. For we kids at McNeal made up only a small portion of the teenage patients he had in hospitals scattered all across Chicagoland. His day began at two or three in the morning when he'd set out from his house in Glencoe and drive from hospital to hospital in his banged-up Mercedes on which the hubcaps were always falling off, *Aida* or *Carmen* playing full blast on his tape deck.

Another reason we idolized him was that once a patient had been sufficiently terrorized and immersed in his system, Schwarz adopted the role of goofy, benevolent dictator and father. Every so often he'd make a surprise visit to the unit and interrupt group therapy to take us all out for ice cream sundaes at the diner across the street from the hospital. Or he'd impulsively pile a few select patients into his cruddy Mercedes and take them out shopping for clothes, charging it all to their parents' bills. Though he'd tell us that his role with us counted for very little now, that what mattered was the daily work we did on the unit with staff and one another, we knew better. We knew that he alone had authority over what we cared about; for only he could sign the okay for our weekend passes or, better still, sign our release from McNeal. When he stepped onto the unit late Friday afternoons, the effect was always electric. "Doc," his slight figure clad in his signature old cardigan and plaid pants, would be instantly swarmed over by kids all vying for his attention, the prettiest girls hanging all over him, pulling flirtatiously on his tie, beseeching him for a weekend pass home.

How I envied the ease the other kids all had bantering with Doc. I alone seemed to be always hanging back, unable to push myself forward. My roommate Indian Brave would even feel free to clown around and tell Schwarz things like, "Doc, you gotta let me outta here, quick. I am getting, like, *so* incredibly horny!" With slim bare feet encased in felt moccasins and eyes slitted with ice-cold confidence, my roommate was clearly the coolest dude on the unit. He'd be at the center of things during free time, the couple of hours before bed when everyone, boys and girls, would sit in the boys' dayroom playing endless hands of pinochle while David Bowie's *Ziggy Stardust* album played over and over on the stereo. I'd use this time to steal back to our room and torture my face with the crazy acne treatment I was still faithfully practicing. Because the sink in our room was right out in the open, a few feet from our beds, I could only be assured of uninterrupted privacy by setting to work on my face during pinochle time. For I would sooner have jerked off in full view of my roommate than let him see me attacking my acne, bloodying towels and swabbing on that stinging alcohol solution that brought the tears to my eyes. By the time my roommate came in I'd be under the covers feigning sleep, my ghastly, screaming-red face turned to the wall. Ironically, I, who slept less than anyone but Schwarz, was thought by my roommate to be a guy who slept ten hours a night.

Since that magical summer with Stephanie when I was twelve, no girl had shown any interest in me, let alone touched me. And yet, amazingly, there were suddenly *two* girls who fancied me. On the otherwise all-white unit it figured that both these girls were minorities. At least I could think of no other possible reason for their interest in me except insecurity about their race. Becky, a pretty Chinese American, and Laura, an even prettier Mexican, had both just been admitted to the ward. Becky was tall and skinny, sort of flat-chested, and wore glasses. She had very pale skin and was a year older than I. At thirteen, Laura was the youngest patient on the unit. She was also the only one of us who came to McNeal not from home but from a juvenile detention center, for unlike us suburban kids she was a self-described "Mexican wetback" whose family had recently moved from Mexico to a tough neighborhood on Chicago's Near Northwest Side.

During free moments here and there throughout the day Laura began to seek me out and sit next to me. She could have been Italian or Greek with her olive skin and thick mane of ringleted dark brown hair. Unlike Becky, who was shy like me, Laura had liquid brown eyes that sparkled with silly impertinence. Laura was somehow at once childish and beyond her years. You could see it in the tight-fitting green T-shirt she wore that had USA printed on it and that revealed a little belly plump with baby fat as well as well-developed breasts. I'd be at the banquet table in the dayroom reading a paperback when Laura would suddenly be at my side, giggling and pestering me. It irritated me and once or twice I made her cry by telling her impatiently that I just wanted to get back to my book, back to *Jaws* or Kurt Vonnegut's *Breakfast of Champions*. Fittingly, I guess, the only Spanish I asked her to teach me then was for "shut up" and "fuck you."

My coldness had nothing to do with Laura—I wouldn't have wanted to talk to any girl who thought she liked me because how could it be for real? It was like a cruel joke or a terrible mistake. And the worst part was that it drew this embarrassing attention to me. I'd worked hard to keep a low profile on the unit but now I had to hear the other boys laughing about how I had a shadow these days (Laura), or about how Becky had stolen one of my shirts from the laundry room and slept with it in her bed. My only hope was that keeping myself as stone-faced as possible would help this whole embarrassing, weird situation to blow over soon.

Instead, something new and terrible began to prey on my

mind. Dr. Schwarz strolled into the room one dawn and told me, "Congratulations! You're going off to Élan just as soon as we can arrange it." Élan was a "long-term treatment facility" located deep in the Maine woods. Schwarz said it was the greatest place, the only truly "effective" place he knew of. The more he raved about it, though, the more Élan sounded like hell on earth, a hundred times more invasive and terrifying than anything taking place here on the unit. The counselors who ran Élan were apparently all grizzled ex–heroin addicts who'd graduated from Daytop, an in-your-face substance abuse program in New York City. The moment these guys detected something funny in you at Élan, a whiff of attitude, a lack of engagement, they didn't hesitate to dump a can of garbage over your head. Or to make you clear whole paths of snow using only a teaspoon. Or to have all the kids in your cabin gather round your bed and wake you up by screaming down into your face that you're an asshole.

All that stood between me and Élan, apparently, was the need to find out whether my father's insurance company would cover a whole year or two at such an expensive, controversial place.

Yet after several weeks of living under the terrible specter of Élan—which haunted my nights and kept me awake, stomach aching—the word finally came that my father's insurance company had refused to cover it. Dr. Schwarz immediately came up with a new long-term treatment facility for me to go to. (Or was this my father's idea? Since I never saw Dad, I could never tell where Schwarz's plans for me left off and Dad's began.) This new place was an institution down in Texas called Brown, I think. Every time Schwarz came barging into the room in the dawn I expected him to tell me to pack my bag for hi ho Texas. But there was still no word. Just how in flux everything was at this time can be seen in letters my sister wrote a friend: "Keith didn't leave, after all. He might get discharged for a week before he leaves for Texas"; "They still haven't heard anything about Keith, so maybe he'll just go to Evanston High this fall."

In August, perhaps because my bed was needed for a new

victim, Dr. Schwarz abruptly released me and sent me home to Dad. My father made it clear that he was taking me back only very reluctantly. I remember standing out in front of his house feeling stunned by the brightness of the golden sunshine everywhere. For the moment at least I was free.

One day a letter arrived from Laura. She said she was still "in jail," still on the unit, that is, and going crazy because she hadn't been out at all since March. Unlike all the other kids she never even got to go home on weekend pass because her family was "all screwed up" and didn't care about her. She still thought about me every night. Did I ever think of her? Or had I already forgotten her? I was probably fooling around with other girls by now, right?

I wrote back right away to say that, yes, I had been seeing a couple girls but that it was nothing too serious. And far from forgetting about her, I did think of her sometimes. In Laura's next letter she told me she was about to be released. It had been decided she would go to live at a "group home" with other teenage girls "whose families are too fucked up to have them around." Her group home was on Chicago's far North Side, near the Thornville El station—not too far from me and Evanston, right? If I was interested in getting together with her, I could give her a call there.

Early in September I gave her a call. We agreed to meet at the Thornville El station and as I stood waiting for her there on the platform it surprised me how my feelings had turned sharper with the weather. The fall chill in the air made everything suddenly more meaningful. When I spotted a dark-haired, feminine figure far up the sidewalk that looked like—yes, was!— Laura, the reality of it all hit me: this girl is coming to meet *me*, a guy who'd never been on a date in his life. Laura looked older and more glamorous. She smelled of delicious perfume. The group home had already given her a clothing allowance and she was wearing a new pair of very crisp-looking dark corduroys and black patent leather shoes with sleek pointed toes. Standing there in rumpled pants and an old pair of sneakers, I wondered all over again what on earth this pretty city girl saw in a suburban loser like me.

Since neither of us had more than a dollar or two, I took Laura back to my father's house. Dad came home from work a little while later, his eyes wide with wonder at the sight of Laura in the living room. When he heard that she and I knew each other from McNeal, his eyes narrowed and I could see the disapproval in the faint smirk on his lips. Later that night my father told me he'd made a new rule: from now on I couldn't have female visitors at the house when he or my stepmother was not there.

The next time I saw Laura it was a damp, strangely foggy day, so dreary that cars had their headlights on in early afternoon. We wandered aimlessly through the fairways of the Evanston Community Golf Course alongside the sanitary canal, finally winding up back in my old neighborhood where it occurred to me we could find refuge in the fort in David Hill's backyard. Perhaps I'd unconsciously been leading us there all along.

Laura said it would be great if we had some tequila. Some lemons and salt too because that's how you drink it in Mexico: you take a slug of tequila, suck on a lemon to take the edge off the tequila, then lick some grains of salt off your wrist. I left Laura in the fort and set out for Poor Richard's, a liquor store just across the Skokie line, three blocks away. A half hour later I returned with no lemons, no salt, and six bottles of beer. In the Poor Richard parking lot an old black guy I approached told me my crumpled dollar bills would only purchase a half pint of tequila, so I'd asked him to get me beer instead.

But Laura didn't seem to mind. She astonished me, in fact, by using her mouth as a bottle opener—I'd completely forgotten that we needed one—prizing off the bottle caps with her back teeth. She said she'd been doing this with Coke bottles since she was a kid, that her teeth had always been so strong she still didn't have a single cavity. Laura was also a good sport about the fort. When we'd first stepped inside it, I saw through her eyes what a junky, musty shack it was, the old sofa and bunk bed crammed in there stinking sourly of mildew. The fort interior—dim, broiling hot in summer, permanently dank—was an ideal climate for rot. But Laura had made herself right at home on the sofa whose broken back made you feel tipped backward as though ready for rocket liftoff.

Once again, as with Stephanie four years earlier, I found myself in a funky, secret, but somehow very sexy place with a beautiful, exotic girl who liked me. But Stephanie and I had never even kissed—"the ways," after all, had consisted only of chastely holding each other. I'd never actually kissed anyone on the lips before. I wasn't at all sure I knew how to do it properly and here with Laura I could feel the ball rolling toward a whole lot more than kissing, toward what I both longed for and feared. Somehow I was certain that Laura, young as she was, had already had sex, possibly lots of it, and that there would soon be no avoiding the moment of truth when I'd have to tell her I was a virgin.

The moment we started making out wasn't preceded by any tentative, awkward eternity in which we gazed meaningfully into each other's eyes before taking the plunge. No, as we were gulping down our third beers, Laura just started getting silly and trying to tickle me. My hand shot out to grab her by the wrist, to try to stop her tickling, and that was it—we fell into each other's arms and our bodies sprang into action, writhing hungrily against each other, rolling this way and that. Instead of kissing her, I nipped at her neck, burying myself in her intoxicating perfume (Jōvan Musk, I would learn). "Stop slobbering on me so much," she said, laughing. She put her lips to mine and then burst out laughing again, saying I kissed "like a jellyfish" and making me watch an exaggerated impression of how I pursed my lips too tightly together. When I opened my lips wider, she slipped her tongue in my mouth, telling me to French-kiss her back, which I did shyly, with none of the whirlybird energy her own tongue had had in my mouth.

Our shirts came off. Laura told me my skin was so smooth, like a girl's. Her skin felt creamy-smooth too, and much hotter than mine. The muscle tone of her body, her back, her shoulders, was so solid and strong. Together, we stumbled over to the bunk bed and fell in a heap onto the cool dampness of the lower bunk's stained bare mattress. The moment of truth had arrived. I told her that I just couldn't seem to unsnap her bra, that, uh, I'd actually never done anything like this before. But Laura didn't seem to be paying attention; she was saying she needed to pee. Just outside the fort lay a dirty sandbox no longer used by children, and after Laura was done out there I went and peed in the sandbox too.

Laura showed me where and how to touch her. Her pubic hair was pleasingly different from my own, as stiff as a brush. When I entered her, she wriggled with pleasure and said, "The best is when it's first going in." Soon she gasped she was coming—once, then again—but no matter how I pumped away I couldn't even get myself to the brink of orgasm. The sensation of intercourse was just too new and different from my familiar masturbation. Afterward, sharing a cigarette with Laura, I heard that the crickets had started up outside. It must be dinnertime . . . or later. It was easy to lose track of time in the fort, since what little light there was came from the tiny crude "window" in a back corner that had been covered over with a sheet. But though I knew my father would be furious with me, there was no way I was going to cut short such a momentous day. Anyway, I forgot all about Dad a few minutes later when Laura and I started fooling around again and this time I got the hang of it, finally managing to come. My coming in her was no problem, Laura said, because she'd just started taking birth control pills. The enlightened counselors at her group home had already given her a copy of *Our Bodies, Ourselves* and, though she'd just turned fourteen, sent her to a Planned Parenthood clinic.

Our love affair over the next several weeks was all the more enchanting because in the dimness of the fort I'd found the one place where I could be free of my hideous face. Just about every afternoon after school, or evening after dinner, Laura would ride the El to Evanston and we'd head straight for the fort. As Sep-

tember wore on, summer drifted in and out and there'd be swel-
tering nights when the sweat dripped off my forehead onto the
mattress just past Laura's head beneath me. We'd pull our sticky
bodies apart as soon as we'd both come. Other nights a deep
autumnal cold came seeping in, silencing the crickets and sending us under the scratchy, sour-smelling wool army blanket. I
hadn't felt so sexually alive since I was twelve. Back then, the
owner of newly urgent hard-ons that I didn't know how to re-
lieve, I'd liked to run after midnight out into the backyard,
where I'd strip myself naked and shinny up a tree in a fever of
horniness. Or I'd jump on my bike, unzip my pants, and ride
back and forth past the sleeping house of a much older, very
pretty neighbor girl, daring to take out and expose my boner to
the thrilling night wind and to her dark upstairs bedroom
window.

The big difference now, of course, was that I was being sexual
with a girl. And Laura's comfortableness with sex—doing it,
talking about it together—made it easy for me to be comfortable
too. She taught me Mexican slang for cock (*bicho*) and cunt
(*crica*), and had a habit of looking at my crotch suddenly as we
walked along, saying she was just curious if "it" was aroused.
Sometimes she'd impulsively throw herself against me and top-
ple us down onto the golf course turf where, as our hands went
burrowing under the bands of each other's underwear, I'd have
to remember to look up to see if a golfing foursome happened
to be teeing off.

I also loved the timeless intimacy of our talks after sex. As
rain drummed on the fort's wooden roof, kicking up the rich
smell of earth in the yard around us, we'd lie huddled under the
army blanket in the lower bunk, carefully passing back and forth
a cigarette whose glowing orange tip was all that could be seen
in the dimness. Laura began filling me in on the whole story of
how she came to be put in the bughouse. Just as had happened
to me, her world got turned upside down the year she was
twelve. Her father suddenly decided the family should leave their
home in Monterey, Mexico, and make a new life in Chicago. A

city named *Chicago*, however, didn't sound too appealing to
Laura. In Mexican slang, *chi* meant "piss" and *cago* meant "to
shit" and, sure enough, in Chicago it seemed like they'd de-
scended into the gutter. The seven of them (Laura had a sister
and three brothers) found themselves squeezed into a three-
bedroom apartment in rough Wicker Park on the Near
Northwest Side of the city. Drugs were everywhere in this
neighborhood. And her new school had such a "violent atmosphere" that she said a black kid "whipped my ass" on the playground for no reason at all. On top of everything else, there was
her father to contend with—he with the temper, the brillian-
tined hair and waxed mustache, and the gun he kept in the
dresser drawer. Her father, like my mother, had grown up in a
family whose affluence had not devolved to him. His family, so
Laura's mother told her, was riddled with homosexuality and
mental illness; one notorious relative had even "got up on a roof
and shot a bunch of people."

When thirteen-year-old Laura began coming home late with
droopy, marijuana-glazed eyes, her father would insist that she
hand her underpants over to him so that he could inspect them
for sperm. Ironically, though, Laura had sex for the first time
only *after* her father went crazy one night and called her a
whore. Laura was taking a bath when he burst into the bathroom, screaming that no *puta* of a daughter was going to turn
the family name to dirt. He grabbed her by the hair, pushed her
head under the water, and Laura worried he might really drown
her. Her screams brought her mother running in to try to in-
tervene. This gave Laura just enough time to jump into some
clothes and run out into the cold February night. But her father
had gone charging out after her, jumping into his old Cadillac
and tracking Laura down a few minutes later in the alley where
she feared he might run her over. She finally lost him by darting
around a corner, climbing a fence, and hiding out in a garage.
By now icicles had formed in her wet hair.

Laura stayed away for several nights, smoking dope in an
abandoned basement apartment that some neighborhood kids

used as a hangout. Her parents reported her to the police as missing, and since this was the third time a missing person report had been filed on her, some kind of law automatically kicked in and when the cops collared her on the street one morning Laura was sent to the juvenile detention center. After a month in captivity she was told she could go home, but Laura said she didn't want to because she still feared her father might try to kill her. So instead she was declared a ward of the state and sent off to McNeal and Dr. Schwarz.

Much as I hated all my acne, I welcomed the new red marks now appearing on my neck: the "hickeys" I was getting from Laura's love bites that proved to the world I was loved. And I loved Laura—so much that she'd become the only thing that mattered anymore. I'd told her so and now each time I saw her, which was just about every day, she'd ask if I still loved her. I'd say yes, and she'd ask why. I'd then feel pressure to keep coming up with new answers: Because of her big brown eyes. Because she was so playful and fun to be with. Because her mane of dark curls had red highlights in the sun. Because she was never fussy, never tired, never boring. Because of her beautiful hands, her slender wrists, her warm, full lips that expressed all her changing moods. As I went on adding to the list, sometimes my answer— that I loved her because of her birthmark, a tan splotch the size of a quarter that straddled her jaw down by her chin; or because of the fine white down along her upper jawbone—would make her shudder and say no, she hated that. But underneath I could tell she was pleased I seemed to approve of everything about her.

Still, sometimes even this wasn't enough and she'd tell me she couldn't meet me tomorrow because this guy had called her up, wanting to get together. My crestfallen face would make her burst out laughing and tell me she was just checking, that if she could make me jealous then that was the real proof of love. But there was no need to check on my jealousy; if anything, it was something I needed to try to hold in check. I made the mistake of asking Laura what the first time she'd had sex had been like, realizing as soon as I said it that I'd stepped into quicksand where I could only be taken deeper into what wasn't good for me. Laura said she didn't like thinking about that time, that it was an older guy who'd taken advantage of her during one of the times she'd run away from home last winter. So how many times had they had sex? Once or twice, three times at most. But he'd never been a boyfriend or anything. The only real boyfriend she'd had besides me was this Polish American guy that she'd never had sex with. He was such a "goody-goody," in fact, that he dumped her one day after hearing around the neighborhood that she'd become a "bad girl."

For a long time I was afraid to ask Laura why she loved me. When I did screw up the courage to ask, her answer—that there was "something noble" about me, "something kind of British," and that "I knew you had something special inside you to give and I wanted to find out what it was"—was as hard for me to believe as it was satisfying to hear.

Yet Laura didn't mention the one thing she must have prized in me above all else: my single-minded devotion to her. She craved attention more than anyone I'd known and in me she'd found someone willing to sacrifice just about everything on the altar of togetherness with her. The mysterious thing, though, is that when she'd first become so attracted to me on the unit at McNeal, I'd given her no indication—quite the opposite!—of being capable of such devotion.

Anyway, without my quite noticing it, every other interest in my life had now fallen by the wayside. I neglected Bryan and my other friends and only one day when I happened to take Laura to the Spot for pizza did I hear from the M.C. there, the guy who'd thought about adopting me for a while the past winter, that I'd become "way too obsessive" about Laura. He told me (Laura had gone off to the bathroom) that just because I had a girlfriend didn't mean I had to give up music. After all, he pointed out, even when I'd been locked up in the bughouse I'd still managed to practice every day in my room.

It was true. I was so obsessed with Laura that it took me completely by surprise when the net came falling down again over her and me. Just before dinner one night the kitchen phone rang and my father handed it to me, saying, with a portentousness he was unable to conceal, "Uh, Keith, Dr. Schwarz wants to talk to you."

It wasn't as though I'd been so "bad" since Schwarz released me. Yes, I'd missed a few days of school here and there, missed more than a few dinners at Dad's. There'd been several nights when I'd stretched the ten-thirty curfew my father had set for me, and in the past few weeks there'd even been nights, cold October nights, when Laura hadn't wanted to go home and I'd smuggled her into my basement bedroom through the little window and then smuggled her back out early in the morning, the windowpane now fogged with frost. But my father never caught us; there hadn't been any big scenes with him at all, no shouting matches. There had been no one terrible moment that cried out to me: Watch it, you're heading for a fall. I felt, if anything, that I'd been juggling things pretty well. After all, this fall semester at Evanston High was the first time I'd done real coursework— read textbooks, turned in written assignments—since I was twelve. The handful of school days I'd cut were due not to Laura but to mornings when I just couldn't bring myself to step outside and show my face in public because it looked so god-awful and ravaged in the bathroom mirror from the searing, crazy acne treatment I'd given it the night before.

Was Dr. Schwarz calling now, I wondered, not so much because I'd failed but because my father and stepmother had tired of me? Though I was too scared of them now to risk provoking any confrontations, things were strained between them and me and always would be, I supposed, even as we politely stepped around one another in the house and did our best to make happy talk at the dinner table.

Only with Laura in the cocoon of the fort or in the deserted green of the golf course alongside my beloved canal did I really feel at home. The hours, the miles Laura and I had logged walking to and from the El station! It seemed like half our time together was spent out in the weather on the golf course fairways—in the warm, mellow luxury of Indian summer, the red and gold trees on the canal bank reflected down in the still water; on freshly minted, crystalline afternoons when it was raining yellow elm leaves; in the misty drizzle with shiny wet leaves sticking to the soles of our shoes; in the poignant dusk smelling of chimney smoke when we could hear migrating geese honking loudly overhead; or late in the evening, hurrying to the station under the cold stars.

Considering how easy it was to lose track of time in the fort, and how Laura never wanted to go back to the group home anyway, I thought I was managing pretty well.

But there was no arguing with the authorities in our lives. When my father handed me the phone I took a deep breath before putting Dr. Schwarz to my ear. Then there it was: the familiar voice, swooping into falsetto and cheerfully crowing at me. "Hello there! Guess what?! The party's over! Oh, yes. You and your Mexican girlfriend are going to stop being naughty and perverting each other and come back in for a nice, long brainwashing."

In order that Laura and I would not continue our destructive influence on each other, Schwarz decided to place us in separate hospitals that he operated out of. Laura went back in McNeal while I got sent to a place called Riveredge. Sprawling and two-storied, "the Edge," as everyone called it, resembled a very large, run-down motel from the 1950s. Each of the many wings represented a different ward. The whole hospital was psychiatric. And true to its morbid name, the Edge overlooked a gloomy river and a small cemetery. This, at least, was the view out back from the intake ward. The view from the adolescent ward I soon got put on was of the forest preserve across the road in front of the Edge. All this surrounding wilderness made me feel imprisoned in the middle of nowhere, a million miles away from Laura, though in fact it turned out we were no more than a few miles apart.

My new ward at the Edge was not quite so regimented as the unit at McNeal; I had time for hours and hours of daydreaming and staring out the picture window in the dayroom. Now that it was November I could see deep into the forest from my second-story perch. The few odd scraps of leaves still hanging on the trees here and there only emphasized the terrible new nudity of the forest. Particularly on a leaden, drenched November day—low clouds misting in thick as soup, the tree trunks oiled with rain, piles and piles of miserable rain-soaked leaves on the ground—it was easy to think the world was ill. The time had just been set back an hour and at four-thirty the day was already dying. By five the nearly full moon was peeking through the witchy trees, rising above them into a sky whistled clean by blustery winds, the moon itself looking stripped clean, coldly glowing with no aura at all, a dead white bone.

Before too long the picture window was fogging up, the air outside thick with swirling snow flurries. Under heavy iron skies, a steady wind was going about ripping off every last wrinkled oak and maple leaf from the branches. The image of Laura that kept coming to mind was of her in the beautiful sweater she'd been wearing the last time I saw her, a cardigan sweater of thick knitted wool the black-purple color of plums; it reminded me of Peruvian Indians and yet seemed so distinctively *her*. I hadn't heard a word from her because Dr. Schwarz had forbidden all communication between us. I'd begun playing my guitar again, working on songs about Laura every day in my room despite hearing that the nurses referred to my doing this as unhealthy "isolating behavior" in their daily charts on me. "The world without you, darling/is so dark I cannot see/inside of me" is how I remember one song going.

On his dawn visits to my room, Dr. Schwarz seemed to relish making me feel terrible about Laura. He said Laura had already forgotten all about me and would be "fucking every guy at McNeal if only she could." Seeing the pain on my face, Schwarz smiled in mock sympathy and said, "Broke your heart, did she?

Oh well, she's fourteen going on forty. Best thing to do is find a nice girl next time."

It didn't take much to make me doubt my worthiness, to return me to my face, my horrible, horrible face. Sitting in the dayroom I'd daydream that I looked like one of the other boys on the ward, a black-eyed guy with skin as clear and white as milk—skin so delicately translucent that, though he was always neatly shaven, a dark, manly beard growth could be seen just beneath the skin. I'd also fantasize that I spoke several languages: I'd be called to the phone in the nurses' station and everyone would gape at me as I burst into French or Italian.

As Thanksgiving came and went my mother began to get fed up with my sitting around in cold storage like this at the Edge. The plan to send me to the treatment center in Texas had fallen through a long time ago and now it had become clear to Mom that Dad's only real plan was to keep me out of his hair at all costs—or rather, at low cost, since it cost him very little to keep me at the Edge. But when my mother made an appointment with Dr. Schwarz and asked him why I was being kept at the Edge, she says Schwarz just rattled off a string of clichés to her, such as that I had "problems with authority and identity." She pointed out that this was true of virtually all adolescents but he had no answer to this except to shrug and throw up his hands as though to say, What can I do?

What Mom did was call up Dad. She raised with him the very idea that she herself had nixed two years earlier—sending me off to New York to live with Uncle Eddie. But though my mother now thought Eddie might be the best person for me after all, my father rejected the plan for more or less the same reasons Mom once had: a young, gallivanting gay uncle could hardly offer a troubled teenage boy like myself the "stable environment" I so badly needed. My father grumbled that, anyway, he was sick and tired of "picking up the pieces" when Mom's schemes fell apart. He didn't appreciate her butting in. He accused her of turning me against him.

Meanwhile Dr. Schwarz, who seemed to feel caught between

my parents, had started acting strangely sheepish around me. The man I'd grown so used to seeing as omnipotent now sounded more like a mere professional my father had hired. "Your father doesn't want you back in the house—or in New York, either, with your uncle. What can we do?" Schwarz added that it was going to take time to cast around for a new long-term treatment center for me seeing as we'd entered the holiday season, when not much work got done in offices across the land. But my mother discovered through her lawyer that she could send Dad and Dr. Schwarz a release order; provided neither of them challenged it, Mom would be free to come to the Edge and collect me. My mother, however, still hadn't checked with Uncle Eddie about whether he still wanted or even remembered wanting to adopt me. Telephoning him in New York one night, she was relieved when Eddie agreed on the spot to take me in.

But now my father flew into action, seeming re-energized by Mom's challenge to his authority. He checked around town and found out that Chicago's Michael Reese Hospital had an adolescent ward willing to keep me locked up for eighteen months—until I'd turned eighteen, that is, and could sign myself out.

Mom and Dad appeared headed for a showdown over me. But instead of feeling any great tension about my fate being decided, I felt pretty much numb about it all. The prospect of life in a new bughouse or in New York with Uncle Eddie both seemed equally unreal. Under my dark cloud of self-loathing, I only knew that wherever I went I'd still be ugly me. And I'd still be without Laura. Just before Christmas Dr. Schwarz told me he'd washed his hands of Laura and sent her to the House of the Good Shepherd convent on Chicago's North Side. Old Motown songs like the Supremes' "Baby Love" and the Chi-Lites' "Oh Girl" began running through my head because only these songs captured the inner-city desperation and doom I felt, the white clouds of winter breath breathed out on the hard, grassless grounds, glittering with broken glass in the sharp winter morning sun, of what I imagined to be Laura's old school in Wicker

Park, an ancient, wicked place looking more like a reformatory with its spiky black iron gates and fences.

It was my mother who seemed to feel all the outrage, drama, and peril of my situation. Though my father had so far failed to respond to her release order for me, Mom worried he was lying in wait for the very morning—January 2—when she would show up at the Edge to have me released; she saw him swooping in at the last minute and, perhaps in cahoots with Dr. Schwarz, carrying me off to Michael Reese Hospital for another year-and-a-half's incarceration. With this in mind, my mother, who loved and always came so alive during emergencies, threw herself into devising an elaborate contingency plan for me. Should my father confront us at the Edge that morning, I was not to run away or try to fight him off or anything. Instead I was to pretend to be cooperative, getting into his car and waiting till we stopped at a certain red light on Martin Luther King Drive. There, I would suddenly spring into action, jumping out of the car and making a mad dash for the lobby of yet another hospital—Mercy Hospital, a Catholic institution run by nuns where my mother had arranged things so that once I reached the sanctuary of Mercy's lobby someone would be ready to whisk me up in the elevator to the top-floor nunnery where I would hide out among the nuns until Mom had determined that the heat was off and the coast clear.

But no drama ensued the morning my mother came to the Edge to have me released. There was no sign of my father in the lobby or of his car in the parking lot. It all went so smoothly it was almost as though Dr. Schwarz had given us his blessing from behind the scenes. During what turned out to be the last time I saw him, Schwarz was nursing a bad sore throat as he paid one of his dawn visits. He seemed weirdly vulnerable without his usual mocking voice, painfully rasping out to me, "You've got to get in touch with your feelings."

Out in the Edge parking lot Mom threw her arms around me in triumph. "We did it, Keithie, we did it! You're free!" Guiltily, I tried to work up some feeling but couldn't. My mother too, as we climbed in her car, seemed to be fighting a sense of hollow anticlimax. She'd been so geared up for a big scene with my father that even back at her apartment with hours to kill before my evening flight to New York, she couldn't quite let go of the atmosphere of teeming dangers she'd imagined would surround our getaway. After arguing with her for nearly an hour about whether it was safe for me to go out for a walk, I finally pulled a guilt trip on her by telling her I was so sick of being locked up that I just had to get out in the open air to taste my freedom.

What I didn't tell my mother was that I'd found out Laura's convent, the House of the Good Shepherd, lay only a few blocks away. Outside on Irving Park Road the January day was bright and frigid. A long stream of white smoke was unspooling from a smokestack, the smoke hanging there suspended against the cold blue sky as smoke never did in warmer weather. All my mother's warnings had succeeded in making me so jumpy about being picked up by a passing squad car that I spent only about five minutes pacing around the convent's high stone wall covered in withered creeper vine before heading back. Laura felt very far away. That night Mom took me to O'Hare Airport where a ticket paid for by Uncle Eddie was waiting for me under an assumed name.

PHOTO BY MARGARET FLEMING

LIFE WITH UNCLE ED

Only during the long cab ride into Manhattan from the airport did the weight of the moment finally hit me. I felt vulnerable and small in the back of the big, jolting taxi as it sped through the night. Outside the taxi window I could make out a hulking industrial structure of some sort: an old railroad trestle, it looked like, a grim skeletal thing of blackened wood and iron. To me it seemed invested with all the scary might of New York City. My position in the world felt so forlorn just then that it was easy to imagine myself standing high up there on the trestle, alone and exposed to the night and the wind.

I'd been instructed to get out at Eighty-sixth Street and Columbus Avenue and call my uncle from the pay phone on the corner. But each time I dialed his number the phone was busy. When I finally got through to him, my uncle sang out that he'd be right down and the dial tone in my ear—had he hung up already?—stunned me a little. I'd been expecting to hear the usual welcoming noises: Hey, you made it! How was the trip?

A minute later, there was my handsome uncle standing in the lobby doorway. His face was beaming; with his smooth, unlined chipmunk cheeks, he looked very innocent and kind. When he called out "Hi!," his brown eyes opened so wide that he looked like a little boy on Christmas morning. It had been a long time, two years, since I'd seen him and he looked different: He'd shaved off his mustache and his dark brown hair was much shorter. His face looked younger, softer, and the neatly ironed flannel shirt he was wearing also looked very soft. When I shook his hand he leaned toward me and planted a little kiss on my cheek, the bristles of his beard hurting a bit as they prickled against all my swollen, tender acne.

It's hard to remember everything about that first night, I was so nervous. My uncle showed me my new room, a narrow little room next to the kitchen that he said used to be the maid's room back in the days when people still had live-in maids. Then we sat at the little kitchen table on hard green metal chairs, drinking tea. Soon we'd filled up the kitchen with clouds of cigarette smoke. Every few minutes the phone on the wall above the table would ring again but instead of letting these calls command his full attention, my uncle remained surprisingly mobile and responsive to me. With phone tucked comfortably between shoulder and jaw, his hands were free to continue lighting our cigarettes and pouring out tea. And even as he purred away indulgently to whoever was on the line—"Ohhh! Mmm-*hmmm*"—his merry eyes were meeting mine and then rolling ceilingward, as though to say, My how this one does go on! It also impressed me how quickly and smoothly he could get off the phone. "Listen, my *nephew's* just arrived," he'd say, eyes smiling complicitly at me.

I'd never heard anyone inject plain speech with this cheerful brand of irony. And yet, off the phone, my uncle's manner with me was disarmingly point-blank and simple. "So I hear your mother bundled you up and stole you out of the bughouse," he said, blinking kindly.

A graceful, blond young man came strolling into the kitchen and my uncle introduced him as his roommate, Keith McDermott. "Came to see the nephew," this new Keith said, playfully I gathered, since there was a barely restrained smile on his lips. His voice was pleasantly clear and reedy. He had clean, boyishly handsome features, with the delicate complexion of a redhead (his blond hair, I noticed, was touched with the slightest bit of red and the beard shadow on his cheeks was orange-blond). I hadn't been aware that my uncle was living with anyone. Or perhaps my mother had told me but it hadn't registered in all the tumult of the past few weeks. In any event I'd never known another Keith before. (My grandmother Delilah, faced with the dilemma of two Keiths now living with her son, solved the problem by designating Keith McDermott "Keith number one" and me "Keith number two.")

Though I was conscious of being looked over that night by my uncle and Keith McDermott, I was actually being scrutinized far more closely than I could have imagined. Keith McDermott had just landed the role of the disturbed teenage boy, Alan Strang, in the Broadway production of *Equus* and as he prepared for his role Keith couldn't resist regarding me—a real-life teenager fresh from the bughouse—as a sort of model. His portrayal of the boy in *Equus* ended up incorporating two odd mannerisms I had in my earliest days in New York: a listless way of walking without swinging my arms, and a tendency to peer at people with a furtive, sidelong glance.

In my first forty-eight hours in New York two things were accomplished that I never would have thought possible: my horrible acne was discussed and professional treatment for it arranged. My uncle raised the whole subject gently with me, though he'd in fact been shocked to see how disfigured I'd become. "Oh, that's it," he'd said to himself as soon as he laid eyes on me, having wondered why my life had gone so dramatically awry since he'd last seen me. He made an appointment for me with a dermatologist at a fancy address off Park Avenue and in the waiting room there I felt like fleeing in embarrassment because none of the other patients seated around me suffered from anything visible, let alone grotesque. I was so grateful when the tall, grave dermatologist examined me with quiet dignity. When I told him about the treatment I'd been giving myself with bloodied towels and stinging Retin A, he said evenly, "You're lucky you still have a face."

The treatment he prescribed called for me to empty a sulfur solution that stank like rotten eggs into a tureen of hot, steaming water each night and then to soak the corner of a towel in it, which I would hold to my face like a hot compress. Almost immediately this stinky potion began working miracles, the hard, angry reds and bruised purples of my pustules dramatically shriveling and fading. There were even small patches of newly minted pink skin emerging here and there. Everywhere I could feel dirty pores itching as they became unclogged and gasped for air.

Though I'd known him all my life, now that I was living with him I realized how little I really knew my uncle. I'd always thought of him as "Eddie" because that's what Mother and Grandmother called him, but in New York no one called Uncle Eddie, Eddie: he was Ed. Uncle Ed was also much stronger looking, much thicker in the chest, than I remembered. When I asked him about it, he said he worked out regularly at the gym now, pumping iron. But I'd never noticed before how his lightly freckled hands, too, were not so much sensitive as sturdy looking like the sturdy rest of him—legs, trunk, shoulders, arms. Every time I saw him from behind he reminded me of a faithful farm horse plodding along.

Though he had this soothing, underlying sturdiness, and though his face could look mild and calm as a Buddhist monk's, my uncle told me he was actually very tense inside. He and I

had the same big, sloping shoulders and he said I should make
a point of remembering several times during the day, as he did,
to relax the shoulders by letting them drop. "Tense people like
us don't even realize how our shoulders are always hunching
up," he explained.

To me the source of his tenseness was obvious: his telephone.
With its constant ringing interrupting everything and, worse,
with the threat always hanging in the air that it was about to
ring again, that telephone would make anyone jumpy. No wonder Uncle Ed's hands were so restless. He had this habit of
continually rubbing his thumb and first two fingers together in
the familiar gesture for money, though with him it seemed to
be completely unconscious, the pulse of his nervous energy.
He'd rub his fingers like this even as he was padding around the
kitchen, cooking or talking on the phone or both. But if he was
listening intently to you, he'd tuck his thumb under his chin and
extend his index finger above the thin, wobbly line of his upper
lip, which sometimes wore a faint smile. And if he happened to
be in between cigarettes, the index finger of his *other* hand would
press itself to his temple, pushing up a fold of skin there. I'd
never seen anyone put both hands on his face so intelligently
before.

But the strangest thing was that though his hands were capable of flying up into graceful gestures when he was talking,
these same hands, I noticed, hung down heavy and clumsy looking during "off" moments when he was just walking silently
along.

As if he hadn't already done enough for me, my uncle handed
me an old leather wallet one morning filled with the first in-
stallment of what seemed like a crazily grand weekly allowance.
I guess maybe it wasn't really all that much but all my life I'd
never had more than a few dollars in my pocket. I couldn't imagine ever needing so much money. And yet, what with my expensive acne medicine and the coffee shop lunches and dinners
I found myself eating when my uncle was busy or out with

friends, I quickly discovered I needed every penny. The Upper West Side in 1976 was very run-down; the city was about to declare bankruptcy and Uncle Ed warned me that many blocks nearby weren't completely safe. The little grocery store half a block north of us on Columbus Avenue had just made an appearance in *Taxi Driver* as the scene where Robert De Niro's Travis Bickle stops a holdup in progress by shooting the robber. And so I was told not to venture too far up or down Columbus and to avoid Amsterdam Avenue completely. If I was heading west to Broadway, I should stick to stately Eighty-sixth Street and never use "shaky" cross streets such as Eighty-fifth or Eighty-fourth Streets.

But I didn't feel like going far. Everything I needed—coffee shop, grocery store, pharmacy—could be found right around the corner. Even so, each time I left the sanctuary of the apartment and stepped out into the crazy kaleidoscope of cars and people on Columbus, I'd feel so overwhelmed I felt like fainting. My eyes would squinch nearly shut against the overload. But soon my uncle was sending me farther afield—to the dentist and to his barber down in the Village. Uncle Ed said there was nothing like a New York haircut; that the haircuts one got in the Midwest were just "hack jobs" and that the Italian barbers here knew how to "layer" hair. It was true; my uncle's barber, Mario, found what seemed to me a new and ideal medium between the crewcuts of my childhood and the corkscrewing mop I'd been carrying around since my Free School days, giving me hair that was manageable yet still long enough to blow in the wind.

One day I discovered that some of my clothes were missing. It dawned on me finally that my uncle must have discreetly thrown the things in the trash, the plaid pair of "Schwarz" pants and two garish floral shirts my mother had bought for me shortly before my release from the Edge. But good taste is as easily acquired as bad by a teenager, and I was soon very attached to the old jean jacket and blue Italian shirt my uncle had given me (we were the same size) as well as the pair of black penny loafers he'd bought me. These were the first "serious" shoes I'd ever owned; the first pair that clacked loudly as I walked, just like characters in European films whose footfalls echoed importantly in halls and courtyards. "Black shoes go with everything," my uncle explained, unlike "dreadful brown."

Even when my uncle was embarrassing me by pointing out that it was never a good idea to wear boxer underpants because they made one's rear end and upper thighs look too bulky, or that I should wear my hair so that it just covered the tips of my ears because my ears, slightly indented at the top, were "funny looking," he'd completely won me over to the unfussy, entirely practical emphasis he placed on the importance of appearance. When I'd asked him why he bothered conforming to the reigning gay clone look of short hair, flannel shirt unbuttoned at the top to expose chest hair, and leather bomber jacket, he charmed me by answering simply, "Because if I didn't, I'd never get laid."

My uncle seemed to be getting laid a whole lot. Almost every night at ten or eleven I'd watch from our sixth-floor windows as he ran out into Columbus Avenue and jumped in a southbound cab, headed for his gay bars down in the Village. I'd be asleep by the time he came home and I always felt bad that what greeted him was a bathroom all stunk up from my sulfurous bedtime acne treatment. But he never said a word, even though his bedroom was right next to the bathroom. Keith McDermott also never complained about it, though he did tell my uncle to "remind" me not to lay my head on the throw pillows when I stretched myself out on the blue living room sofa, reading. Keith had apparently detected the faint smell of sulfur on the pillows recently. But my uncle also relayed words from Keith that thrilled me: Keith said he found me to be "aware of so many different levels." Keith was now playing seventeen-year-old Alan Strang every day in *Equus* rehearsals but around me he'd mischievously taken to referring to himself as "Mom." Like a cat he was playful but poised, with a natural elegance that shone through even the wrinkled white painters' pants and old T-shirts he wore around the house. In a pattern I could never predict, Keith could be open, sly, and distant by turns.

I'd learned to stay out of Keith and my uncle's way during the day—they were too busy for me to be taking up more than a few minutes of their time here and there. Often my uncle would suggest I go out and get some air and exercise, see the city, and though I would dutifully leave the apartment, surprised each time by the glimpse of my new self in the full-length mirror at the head of the hallway near the door, I'd return a short while later, exhausted from my walk around the block. Before long my uncle was joking about my "torpor"—the way I spent most of the day in sickly reading on the sofa.

My uncle blamed everything—the torpor, the fearfulness, the funny mannerisms Keith McDermott had noted—on my long incarceration in the bughouse. Twenty years earlier, in the 1950s, when Uncle Ed was a teenager growing up in Evanston, he himself had nearly been institutionalized at age fifteen. One day his mother had told him she was thinking of marrying "Ham," the newspaper man she'd been dating for several years, and Ed rashly replied, "Then it will have to be a double wedding because I'm going to marry his son." The whole story of Ed's secret love affair with Ham's handsome nineteen-year-old son came out and Delilah was so scandalized that she immediately sent Ed to a local psychiatrist for evaluation. This psychiatrist pronounced Ed "unsalvageable" and recommended he be locked away for good. But in the end Ed was sent off to boarding school instead where twice a week he saw a psychoanalyst named Dr. Moloney who treated homosexuality as the symptom of an underlying but curable neurosis. Three years of treatment with Moloney, however, only succeeded in teaching Ed to doubt his every thought and instinct, since Moloney held that as a "sick" person Ed mustn't trust his own mind.

The rage my uncle still felt toward Dr. Moloney must have been what fueled the fervor I heard in his voice whenever he'd start berating "that monster"—as he'd taken to calling my Dr. Schwarz. For though he'd never met Schwarz, Uncle Ed acted like he knew him all too well: Schwarz was an "egomaniac" who lorded over his teenage patients "like some self-anointed Sun King."

The remarkable thing is there *were* some pretty striking similarities between our two shrinks. Both Schwarz and Moloney shared a love of holding forth and a lack of curiosity unbecoming in a psychiatrist. And each doctor saw so many patients that he was often half-asleep or falling asleep and had trouble remembering people's names, though each would probably have dismissed this as a minor, even irrelevant quibble, since both men administered their therapy in the belief that a patient's personal details, whatever they might be, would merely have turned out to confirm their general theories. But the worst thing about our shrinks is that they failed to understand what really ailed my uncle and me—even as they insisted that they alone knew how to cure us. My uncle's real problem was simply that he happened to be a sensitive boy struggling to come to terms with his homosexuality in the repressive 1950s. As for me, I still can't understand how my horrible acne managed to go untreated as well as unconsidered by Dr. Schwarz and his staff as a possible cause for all my miserable defiance. But as much as our doctors might have been "monsters," my uncle and I were each too haunted by our own demons—he by homosexuality, me by acne—to notice it at the time. He and I were, if anything, deeply vulnerable to the paternal authority of our shrinks because we both felt fatherless for all real purposes as well as so shamefully freakish that we honestly considered ourselves unworthy of the human race.

On the other hand, my uncle and I had each made things worse for ourselves by acting flip with the diagnostic shrinks we'd been sent to see. The day he was declared "unsalvageable" Ed had just finished reading Oscar Wilde's *Lady Windemere's Fan* (Wilde was to blame, in fact, for getting Ed in hot water in the first place, for the "double wedding" quip had been tossed off to his mother very much under the spell of the contagious Wildean impertinence). In the Evanston office of the diagnostic shrink, Ed had finished the job by answering every earnest psychiatric question with little quips delivered in a snippy British accent.

Twenty years later it was my turn to be flip, though in my case it was reading Kurt Vonnegut that put the devil in me. One day at McNeal Dr. Schwarz had sent us patients in one at a time to be evaluated by a stone-faced woman with hair coiled in a severe blonde bun. She'd asked me to draw a stick figure of a man and, when I'd done so, to tell a story about "him." Looking down at my homely stick man, I found myself saying that he lived in a "double outhouse." I'd just finished reading Vonnegut's *Breakfast of Champions* and the story I began to spin off the top of my head was full of the Vonnegut relish for screwball characters happily wallowing in bathroom humor.

A week later I discovered my moment's whimsy had been analyzed with deadly seriousness. Dr. Schwarz let me read the woman's report on me and my eyes went right to the last sentence: "Long-term treatment is recommended in a structured environment."

Too late I learned from my mother that in this particular test all comments about the stick man were seen as revealing one's innermost feelings for Daddy. Dumb me. I'd taken the stick man exercise at face value, treating it as a genuinely blank slate that I was being invited to get creative with. But the baffling thing is that for all the shenanigans I'd subjected my Daddy/stick man to, the report identified my *father* as the parent I felt was essentially "in my corner." This "finding" was so at odds with reality, with everything I was saying about my father in daily group therapies on the ward, that it was soon forgotten by the staff.

My most memorable moment of therapy, as it turned out, occurred when a burly "mental health worker" took me down to the hospital basement one day and handed me a medicine ball. "Okay," he said, "we're going to toss this back and forth and you're going to pretend I'm your dad." As he chanted things at me like, "Keith, I can't have you in the house anymore, you're sick, you're sick, Keith," I dutifully answered him back. But it all seemed so ludicrous. He looked and sounded so little like my

father that I worried my performance here was going to be so
lame that he'd write in my patient's log that "Keith Fleming is
not in touch with his feelings," one of the worst things that
could be said of a patient. But then a miracle happened. Heaving
that heavy leather medicine ball back at him again and again was
getting me so sweaty and irritated that a blind, boiling anger
suddenly erupted out of me and he became my father. "I am *not*
sick!" I yelled. "I'm sick of *you*! I'm sick of how you don't *understand* anything! I'm sick of how you keep locking me *up* in all
these fucking places!" I was trembling and crying and snot was
pouring out my nose. The staff hailed it as my big breakthrough
and it was all thanks to the medicine ball.

My uncle's willingness to look after me was all the more extraordinary given how poor he was. When I arrived in New York in
early January 1976 he had just turned thirty-six and was the
author of a single published book, *Forgetting Elena*, a novel that
had sold only a few hundred copies but had miraculously managed to be singled out for praise by Vladimir Nabokov. Though
Uncle Ed would soon be at work on *The Joy of Gay Sex* and
Nocturnes for the King of Naples, two books that would make his
name, when I came to live with him he was making ends meet
by ghostwriting a U.S. history textbook. I'd assumed I would
attend the local public school but my uncle surprised me by
saying he wanted me to go to an expensive private one. Yet
because my academic record was so riddled with holes from my
unaccredited Free School years and my time in the bughouse,
my uncle discovered that the only way to get me into prep
school was first to send me for a semester at an even more expensive remedial place called the Tutoring School. My mother
agreed to help out with a monthly check, but my father not only
refused to contribute toward any of my expenses but even balked
at sending us my transcript, which we needed to get me admitted
into any new school. Only after Uncle Ed called up my father
and stepmother in a cold fury was the transcript finally sent.

    Over the next few months, whenever the burden of meeting

all my expenses seemed overwhelming, my uncle began suggesting I sue my father. Children suing their parents had just come in vogue and my uncle said he'd been inspired by a magazine article about a Maryland teen who had won damages *and* a divorce from his parents. Uncle Ed had fought a protracted battle as a teenager with his own remote, uncomprehending father to get him to pay for prep school, but *his* father had at least ended up caving in. My father, however, was so stingy that my mother suspected that one reason he'd taken over the custody of us three kids was the small savings he would enjoy by no longer having to pay child support.

But after thinking it over I told my uncle that I just didn't think I was up to suing my father, that I'd rather go to a public high school if prep school was something we couldn't afford. In retrospect, I see that I probably should have tried to get a court to order my father to contribute to my welfare. At the time, however, my still considerable self-hatred (Am I really worthy of a prep school?) mingled with feelings of timidity and shyness (Do I really have a case? Am I really ready for the "spotlight" of playing, in a courtroom, the role of avenging son?) I should have focused more on my poor uncle's feelings and less on my own.

On my father's list of objections to my moving in with Uncle Ed, number one must have been that in such an abnormal atmosphere I might turn gay. But my sexuality turned out to be one of the few things about myself that I couldn't, wouldn't change and gay sex one of the few things about gay men I wasn't interested in trying to imitate. Never before had I met men in their thirties and forties who looked so young and acted so lively, lighthearted, and curious. For though I might have been the only genuine teenager in my uncle's world there seemed to be no lack of "kids," as Ed and his friends all enjoyed calling one another ("Drink up, kids"; "Well, kids, it's been fun"). These friends of Uncle Ed's all seemed to regard me and my presence in the apartment as a real curiosity. Back then in the seventies it was almost unheard of for a gay man, particularly one so young and undomestic as my uncle, to adopt a child. More than a few people, searching their minds for any comparable situation, hit upon the same example—Ed and I reminded them of the off-beat uncle-nephew duo in the Jason Robards movie *A Thousand Clowns*.

More than I knew, I was starting to accept my uncle and his ways as being the norm. My old mumbling way of speaking, particularly on the phone, had so much given way to vocal inflections I'd picked up from Uncle Ed that my mother and grandmother were always mistaking me now for him when I answered the phone. But then I brought a Tutoring School classmate home for lunch one day and saw my uncle anew. This lunch was actually Uncle Ed's idea; he'd heard me mention Richard, a good-looking, curly-haired but rather ordinary kid who, if not a friend exactly, was someone with whom I'd gotten on speaking terms outside class and sometimes grabbed a sandwich at the deli. That morning my uncle told me as I'd set out for school, "Don't worry, I promise not to act too gay," but the moment Richard and I arrived for lunch I found myself embarrassed to be *feeling* embarrassed. "Hi, Richard, let me take your coat," my uncle sang out, extending a hand instead of giving Richard the peck on the cheek a young gay visitor and even I myself could usually expect.

"My nephew's told me all about how great you are," my uncle went on, gesturing for Richard to sit down on one of the green metal kitchen chairs. Uncle Ed seemed to have decided that lunch in the humble kitchen would be more comfy—more *straight*, I guess—than the kind of luncheon he'd serve his own friends in the dining room, all flowers, and ratatouille and ice water in crystal pitchers. But as my uncle whisked the batter for our cheese soufflé I saw how hopelessly awkward the situation was, how despite all efforts to rein himself in his face and voice would always be too animated for someone like Richard, the compliments too over-the-top. I realized all over again how theatrical my uncle was. He and his friends had evolved a manner that could be very much like being onstage, with every sentence uttered a potential "line" and every facial expression a clear, even exaggerated, register of what was being felt.

Now that I knew about my uncle's near miss with institutionalization as a teenager I could see how he might identify with me a bit. But what I never could have suspected is that by moving in with him I was in any way helping *him*—but that's just what he proceeded to tell me one night.

My uncle's relationship with Keith McDermott was something I'd been struggling to understand. Although they slept in separate bedrooms, I'd assumed at first that they were "a couple" in the way that everyone I'd ever known defined the concept. But as I heard Keith and Ed talk in each other's presence about their outside sexual escapades (they both joked about knowing the number of the pay phone down below our windows so that they would be ready to ring it if a cute "trick" happened to be walking past), I began to think things between them were merely merry and casual. Only now, this particular night, did I finally see how painful their relationship often could be for Uncle Ed, for he confided to me that by coming to live here I'd been helping to distract him from how miserably in love he'd fallen with Keith.

I guess anybody could have been confused about the true nature of my uncle's feelings for Keith—particularly if he'd listened to Ed espouse day after day, as I had, a gleefully modern philosophy involving the "compartmentalization" of love and sex and friendship as practiced by him and his fellow gay New Yorkers. As Ed would sum it up in his book *States of Desire:* "Sex is performed with strangers, romance is captured in brief affairs, friendship is assigned to friends." The funny thing, though, is that what my uncle seems to have longed for with Keith is just the kind of long-term romance that his philosophy of love had so breezily dismissed. But the problem was that Keith, while loving Ed as a friend, did not feel physically attracted to him.

Now that my uncle had revealed to me how he suffered over Keith, I could see how even the bedroom Keith occupied reflected his powerful yet aloof status in the apartment. For while my uncle's room was next to the bathroom and not much bigger than my own little maid's room, Keith slept in the master bedroom off the front hallway. The door to his room was always kept shut and I only got to visit the room once or twice. It seemed all the bigger for its bareness, for I can't remember much furniture besides the big foam cube in the middle of the room that he slept on.

Which was worse? I wondered. To love someone who lived with you but didn't love you, or to love someone whom you might never see again—someone who probably didn't even know where you were? I suspected that the girls in the House of the Good Shepherd convent were not allowed to correspond with boyfriends, but just in case Laura might be able to sneak out a letter to me, I asked my mother to drop off my new address with a nun at the front desk there. This dazzling New York address of mine—76 W. 86th St, Apt. 6-C 10024—was something I could admire for several minutes before finally depositing my letter in the mailbox. The one pure joy I took in living in New York, in fact, was imagining how impressed my old friends must be by such an address. In an insufferable letter I wrote to the kids in my old Evanston neighborhood, I declared:

> It's hard to concentrate with my uncle's roommate, also named Keith, shouting out the lines of his forthcoming play *Equus* in which he's co-starring with Richard Burton of alcoholic fame. You know, it's funny how Chicago seems like a huge, expensive imitation of Akron, Ohio. I now believe New York to be the only point of civilazation in a vast land of barbarians.

I'd heard my uncle playfully refer to the rest of America outside Manhattan as "the provinces." Soon I was egging him on, getting him to fill me in on all the differences between provincial people and New Yorkers—such as that provincials watched TV all the time whereas New Yorkers like Uncle Ed didn't even own a television. Or that New Yorkers didn't own cars (which my uncle disdainfully referred to as "autos," pronouncing the "t" so that it came out "aw-toes"), those contraptions that provincials "spend half their lives in," driving the things to work under "raw dawn skies." No, New Yorkers walked everywhere. They walked fast, talked fast, and panicked whenever they found themselves more than a block away from a pay phone or subway station. And New Yorkers would never dream of dining earlier than eight in the evening. For what seemed to irk my uncle more than anything about the provinces was the bleak six P.M. dinners eaten in "shameful silence" out there; those poor people were so understimulated in their lonely, dimly lit suburbs that Uncle Ed said their lives were not just sad but "unhealthy." All that he could find to like about the American countryside were "those beautiful silver grain silos."

At the little dinner parties my uncle hosted at the apartment I began to hear myself snippily dismissing Chicago even as I knew in my heart that I found New York intimidating and in fact missed the Windy City and my friends there. But my uncle's example had led me to discover in dinner party opinions a kind of alternative reality where one could have fun posing as more heartless and haughty than one ever really was beneath one's skin. Hadn't Uncle Ed said that at the dinner table it was more important to be interesting than truthful—that one often needed to "embroider on the truth"?

Still, it could be hard sometimes for me to know what Uncle Ed genuinely believed, since he was capable of contradicting himself over the course of the same dinner party. Early on, for instance, I'd hear him complaining about the way midwesterners had of dithering over everything, including saying good-bye, which irritated him no end when he was visiting out there because he didn't want another hug, didn't want to say "Well, you take care now," and longed instead to get away with a simple, crisp good-bye the way New Yorkers do. But an hour and three glasses of white wine later he'd have switched to praising midwesterners and attacking New Yorkers. Now he would be describing himself as "a good, public-library midwestern intellectual" who was sick of meeting "Princeton-educated New Yorkers who've majored in Cocktail 101 and have opinions about everything but never really read anything."

Most nights at the apartment, though, were quiet school nights. I'd be doing my homework at the kitchen table at ten in the evening as Uncle Ed, hair gleaming from a shower, dressed in leather bomber jacket and jeans, said good night to me as he headed out the door for another night of cruising down in Greenwich Village. I was fascinated by this shadowy world of sex he kept disappearing off into. Though his favorite bars had names like the Toilet and the Anvil, it all struck me as rather glamorous if only because that's how my uncle looked as he left the apartment. Then one Sunday afternoon I happened to visit the west end of Christopher Street with him and was astounded by the crowds of men lining the stoops and sidewalks; wall-to-wall eyes, as I uncomfortably felt it. It was explained to me, after I'd asked, that a man wearing a red bandana in his right back pocket advertised himself as submissive, in his left pocket as dominant, while a yellow bandana meant the owner was into "golden showers."

The funny thing is that Uncle Ed was so blasé about all the sex he was having that in our daily talks in the kitchen he and I came up with something we called "the icky system." This was a system that rated the quality of Ed's sex with various people based on the idea that all sex is to some degree icky. Because the icky system awarded only negative scores, the highest rating that could be bestowed on his sex with someone was "minus one icky" (the rating he gave Keith McDermott), though more par for the course was, "Oh, I think the guy last night must have been minus four or maybe even minus five ickies."

Despite the demands of his nightlife, which often kept him out till two in the morning or later, my uncle had decided he should make an effort to be present at breakfast before I went off to school. One morning, however, I failed to rise from my bed in the maid's room. The insomnia I'd developed in the bughouse while tossing and turning with worry each night about being sent to that frightening place in the Maine woods had stayed with me, and on this particular morning my uncle ended up carrying my breakfast in on a tray that he placed beside my bed. Even so, I was so groggy that morning that when he looked in a moment later I still hadn't raised my head from the pillow.

Seating himself on the edge of my bed, he cooed sweetly, "Wake up, Nephew, wake up."

". . ."

"Or maybe I should join you under the covers, mmm?"

". . . ?!"

"No? Of course not. How about some scrambled eggs with your toast?"

If my uncle was an experienced seducer, he was equally experienced at rejection—something I was certainly wide awake by now to appreciate! But there was no aftermath to this gentle, entirely verbal little come-on from him. And I think of it as having been a verbal thing. That rash remark my uncle had made as a teenager to his mother about the "double wedding" was something that he would always see as having just unaccountably popped out of him (though one could argue that he'd gotten his loose tongue from his own mother's example, Delilah being someone who'd actually confided once to eight-year-old Eddie that his father's penis was surprisingly small). Anyway, my uncle's remark to me in bed that morning was again something that I think just somehow popped out of his mouth. Whatever it was, it had all happened in the wink of an eye, and was just as quickly gone from the realm of possibilities. It had been an intensely awkward passing instant, it's true, but it was also something I promptly forgot about, as did he, like a crazy dream dreamt just before waking. All that mattered to me was that there would be no lingering awkwardness and that our relationship would continue on unchanged—which is exactly what happened.

Then too, as an "acne survivor" what most haunted me then was that I was still ugly; any passing nod to my attractiveness was thus something that, if not always exactly welcome, was never altogether displeasing. In fact, when a famous gay poet visited the apartment one day I discovered that I felt only flattered to learn that he had been interested enough to ask Ed later, when they were alone, whether I too "shared the family taint."

Gradually I told my uncle all about Laura. How we'd met. How pretty she was. How she was walled up in a convent now. But the first thing I remember him saying to me about her was, "You know, you're not pronouncing your girlfriend's name correctly, by the way. A lot of people say 'Lora,' as you do, but it's actually supposed to be pronounced *LAW-ra*." My uncle smiled to show me he was aware how stuffy this sounded to the modern American ear, but a moment later he was adding that people also tended to mispronounce his own name. "People say *White* as though there's no 'h' in it. They make the same mistake with *which*, pronouncing it *witch* instead of" (and here he demonstrated the proper, aspirated "h" sound that had been lacking). But Uncle Ed was full of all sorts of other interesting tidbits about English that I've put into practice ever since. He said that in general one should speak of *this* and not of *that*, of *this* book, *this* man, "Because it's almost as though the world is more real and closer to hand for rich or educated people. It's the poor and powerless who are always saying 'that book,' 'that man,' because they see these things as farther away, beyond their control."

I learned about the "distinction that's often forgotten now" between *eager* and *anxious* (we're eager to see our lover, anxious about seeing the dentist) as well as the one between *jealous* and *envious* (we're jealous of what we have but fear losing, envious of what we don't have but covet). I learned that one should write *okay*, not *OK*; *all right*, not *alright*; *normality*, not *normalcy*. From my uncle's example I saw that that the dictionary was not just something to consult wearily when one was stumped but a gold mine to go digging in. I'd be chatting with him in his book-lined study when Uncle Ed would suddenly rise from his writing desk to stoop over the fat Webster's dictionary that sat heavily flipped open on a stand. "Oh, listen to this," he'd say, giggling over a word he'd found. "*Testudinal*: 'of or like a tortoise.' " And on the spot he made up a sentence that got us both laughing: "My dear, I'm afraid your response to my love has been all too testudinal."

The second thing my uncle had said on the subject of Laura was, "Well, I think you've got to read *Lolita* and *Swann's Way*." Nabokov's masterpiece and the opening section of Proust's great work happened to be Uncle Ed's two favorite books, but I think what he had in mind for me was their common theme of obsessional love. Anyway, as a boy whose reading had consisted mostly of Kurt Vonnegut novels, I sure did feel in over my head as I lay on the blue living room sofa reading a bit of *Lolita*, a bit of *Swann's Way*. My letter to my friends in Evanston shows what a mishmash I was making of this fancy new reading.

> I was reading Nabokov and he said people are always telling him they fall in love with the wrong people. Well, according to Nabokov that's exactly what falling in love means, with the wrong person.

What makes this such a whopper is not just that I'd attributed to *Nabokov* the very Proustian notion of falling in love with the wrong person. No, this loving-the-wrong-person notion wasn't even something I'd gleaned from my reading—it was something I'd heard my uncle say that I'd promptly gotten mixed up in my mind. I myself was too occupied with just trying to navigate through the sheer daunting style of *Lolita* and *Swann's Way* to be able to boil any of it down into such a pithy summation.

But another book my uncle suggested I read, Lord Chesterfield's *Letters to His Son*, made immediate sense to me. These letters from an eighteenth-century father to his illegitimate teenage son cover—in very cynical, exacting detail—all that a "gentleman of fashion" should know. As I read through the book, I kept recognizing my uncle. In the passage on the art of flattery, for instance, Chesterfield says that beautiful people are best flattered by being told they're brilliant, and brilliant people that they're beautiful. This dictum was something I'd often seen my uncle putting into practice. Ditto for the dictum that a gentleman never rises later than ten in the morning, no matter when he might have gone to bed, and that his day should be divided evenly between study and pleasure, which mutually refresh each other. Or that a gentleman makes use of every minute of the day, including his time on the toilet (just as Chesterfield recommended, my uncle occupied himself with lighter reading while in the john). Or that fruitfully employing one's time includes any and all socializing, the only real sins being idleness and gracelessness. The Chesterfieldian insistence on the importance of charm and easy, elegant manners—what he calls "the graces"—all spoke to me of my uncle. For if social skills really are the most important thing we can possess, my uncle was someone so unendingly sociable that Keith McDermott told me that even when Ed was sleeping his face wore a faint smile.

Letters to His Son revealed to me that more than anything my uncle had styled himself after an eighteenth-century man of the world. Because though Uncle Ed indulged himself in vast social and sexual lives, the code he actually lived by put more emphasis on self-discipline than hedonism. He would tell me from time to time that it was probably difficult for a young person like myself to grasp the hard work going on beneath what must look like a life devoted to fun, but I knew how hard he worked. After school, as I lay reading on the living room sofa, I'd hear him hammering out his U.S. history book on the typewriter in his study that was dominated by a framed picture of a dead-serious Nabokov staring out with formidable, piercing eyes.

My uncle had also started writing his novel *Nocturnes for the King of Naples*, but this was something he preferred to "compose," the word he always used, by hand on thick sheets of paper using a beautiful fountain pen. As he wrote, his telephone would keep ringing with yet another call from yet another friend checking in or making plans for the evening, and I came to know the glamour of such a busy, popular telephone (and consequently, the shame of the quieter phones I'd known in the Midwest). Yet my uncle imposed discipline on his love of conversation, limiting each phone chat, however amusing and punctuated by his deep, wonderfully wicked laughter, to a brisk five minutes. The real secret to his being able to have so much fun *and* get so much done, I decided, resided in his energy. As I lay on the sofa staring into space, *Lolita, Letters to His Son*, or *Swann's Way* on my chest, I'd find myself thinking that were a movie to be made of my uncle's life the cameras would hardly ever need to stop rolling, so much did he seem to be perpetually "on," socializing and writing and throwing himself into every minute of the day.

If there was glamour to his busy phone, there was magic in the music continuously playing on his dusty, disheveled record player. One after another the beat-up discs of Handel's Concerto Grosso would plop down from where they hung stacked above the turntable—a mechanism that my uncle reminded me actually fell within the robot category. It was easy to see why he used the word *compose* to refer to his novel-writing because music was palpably his favorite art. For just as had happened to Keith McDermott when he first moved in, I too was learning under my uncle's influence to love "serious music" and to discover how a perpetual Brahms and Bruckner background gave an ordinary afternoon a much-needed boost, supplying it with soaring heroism and sadness and making me feel that my own emotions were being deepened and improved. When Uncle Ed had been a teenager reading novels while his father worked at his desk, the Brahms and Mahler records his father played had been the only thing they had in common, something my uncle had even hoped might constitute a "shared rapture" between him and his impassive father. I myself saw the music we listened to while my uncle worked at his desk not so much as our shared rapture (he gave of himself enough that I didn't need to grasp at such a lonely consolation) but rather as the outward presence of the magic contained in the writing he was doing.

"Do you mind if I read you something?" my uncle started asking me late in the afternoons, stepping out into the living

room through the opened glass double doors of his study. I'd
feel flattered as well as inadequate as he stood there reading
freshly written pages from his *Nocturnes*. I didn't realize that in
his excitement it didn't really matter who the audience was. I'd
sit there straining to attune myself to this novel he'd told me
was "surreal, total fantasy" but that I couldn't help recognizing
was filled with Keith McDermott, my grandparents E.V. and
Delilah, and Ed himself. My uncle's reading voice took some
getting used to, being higher and more prissily precise than his
everyday voice. And if he happened to be in the midst of a particularly beautiful passage, his voice could get so reverent and
soft that it wasn't always completely intelligible above the surging arias of Bizet's *Pearl Fishers* playing on the stereo. With his
raised eyebrows and gently blinking eyes, he made me think of
one of those older choir boys standing a head taller behind the
younger boys. These beautiful passages in *Nocturnes* featured lots
of what my mother referred to as "those flights of poetry Eddie's
always sailing off into"—flights she said she skipped when reading his stuff so as to get back to the story. But though these
flights usually sailed right over my head, my uncle, sensing
sometimes that I might not have got it, would look up and explain, for instance, that the "ruined cathedral" was based on an
abandoned warehouse along the Hudson where he went cruising
sometimes, and that he had in mind a gigantic bird when he
wrote "Soaring above me hung the pitched roof, wings on the
downstroke . . ."

But what made me most tense was the funny parts. I knew
my uncle welcomed and even expected his audience to laugh out
loud in all the right places, and it worried me that I might be
letting something amusing slip past. Fortunately, I found I could
usually take my cue from his voice, which would slow down to
drawl out with special relish anything he intended to be hu-
morous, and from his lips, which in the slight pause that followed would pucker in suppressed merriment. And fortunately
the scenes my uncle found most hilarious were the same ones
I'd already be laughing at automatically. In *Nocturnes* my sober

Cincinnati grandfather, E.V., had been transformed into a drug-addled playboy who idles away his time in the south of Spain surrounded by a collection of adult dependents he calls "the time-wasters." When my uncle reached the part where this father is sometimes spending "a quiet evening at home with just heroin, a few records and the enema bag," the reading had to come to a halt for a minute as the author shook with that wonderful wicked laughter and brushed away the tears with his sleeve.

Now that I understood him better, I saw how concealed behind my uncle's warm, all-purpose sympathy was a highly critical, astringent mind. And so though I'd learned from his example to hear out even the most crashing bore at a party with nodding encouragement, I also learned to ridicule self-indulgent pop therapy for devoting so much energy to making people feel better that it was being forgotten that such a thing existed as *actual guilt.* Uncle Ed also taught me to scorn the notion of the artist as too beautiful for this world—as too exquisite to keep practical affairs in order or remain emotionally stable. More than once he advised me never to become a writer, to become a businessman instead, because writers were so poorly paid. If I must be a writer, he suggested I satirize flaky creative types instead of the usual bourgeois targets.

It might seem that my uncle was simply pouring his opinions into my impressionable young mind, but this would leave out my own feeling that something dormant within me had been awakening and responding to his sensibility. I was not simply a passive audience but someone who constantly egged him on, quizzing him so much that once he grew exasperated enough to tell me, "You think I have all the answers." For my Tutoring School English class I wrote a term paper comparing the wildly different notions about love held by the psychologist Erich Fromm and the French writer Stendhal. I'd become a fan of Stendhal's *Love* after hearing my uncle praise it, but it was my own idea to favorably contrast Stendhal's passionate, literary observations with the workaday, unexciting ones of Fromm's *Art of Loving.* My uncle helped me type my paper up but the words were all mine. I remember how pleased I was when he exclaimed at one point, seeming genuinely impressed, "This really is pretty good."

On the other hand my guitar playing, such a big part of my identity, was now through my uncle's influence a thing of the past. But this was my own decision, not anything he advised me to do. Uncle Ed had actually made a few stabs at encouraging my "folk music," as he called it, listening politely as I sang him some songs in the kitchen with its ringing acoustics. Afterward, the only comment I remember him making was, "I've always thought it would be so interesting to write a song where the lyrics are totally at odds with the melody. You know, have these dead-serious words set to a tune that's very jaunty. Or have a haunting melody where the lyrics are all very lightweight, like champagne bubbles." When the elevator man in our building suggested I take lessons from a venerable Harlem jazz guitarist he knew, my uncle said we could probably afford one lesson every couple weeks. But with all he was already doing for me, guitar lessons seemed like a luxury that my uncle couldn't afford and I didn't deserve. There was one time, just one time, when I happened to play one of my own records on the stereo—an album by Chicago singer-songwriter Steve Goodman, I think it was—and my uncle came out of his study to tell me politely, "You know, I don't really mind what you play so long as it doesn't have English words in it. Sorry, it's just that I find it sort of distracting when I'm writing."

When Uncle Ed told me that our Armenian landlady, an eccentric old bird who lived in the apartment directly beneath us, had complained to him about "all the thumping going on up there lately," I knew the time had come to put away my guitar for good. It was all just getting too embarrassing. I'd had no idea I was in the habit of stomping out the time with my right foot while playing the guitar. Though my uncle had never said in so many words that folk music was not worthy of my time, I felt it in the air by implication. I mean, didn't it all follow very logically? If my hometown and thus my whole life till now was provincial, and if Kurt Vonnegut was, as my uncle confided, "strictly an adolescent author," then what did this say about my music?

Still, there turned out to be limits to how much I'd let myself be reshaped. My name, for instance. Out of the blue one night my uncle brought up the idea of legally changing my name to Keith White. I told him I thought "Keith Fleming" sounded slightly better than "Keith White," thinking he was just being fanciful about the whole thing. Only later did I learn he'd been very serious about it and hurt by my rejection. But I think I would have stuck with Keith Fleming in any case because with so much of me in flux I needed to at least hold on to my name. "Keith White" just sounded too alien, like another person.

One day after school I found a letter from Laura on the kitchen table. She wrote that she was so glad I remembered her because she'd worried she'd lost me forever. She hoped I still loved her. Right before Christmas Dr. Schwarz had stuck her in this stinking convent, after threatening for weeks to send her off to a hard-core reformatory for girls in Geneva, Illinois, where he told her the inmates were all "dykes and sluts with smelly snatches." She asked if Schwarz had said anything to me about her, because Laura's second time in McNeal had "really sucked"; Schwarz kept putting her in the isolation room where she couldn't even scratch her ass because she was tied down in restraints. And one day Schwarz poked his head in and told her with a gloating smile, "Keith is going off to live in New York, you know. Oh, yes! But you're staying right here." Laura got the feeling Schwarz was glad he'd broken us up because I, as a middle-class white kid, was "too good" for her. But that wasn't true, was it? Somehow we'd think of a way to be together again, wouldn't we?

When my uncle came into the kitchen to make more tea he asked what Laura had to say. I told him everything except the be-together-again-someday part, and he said Schwarz should be

stripped of his license and made to experience one of his own
hellholes. Later that day my uncle and I went to see the new
Truffaut film, *The Story of Adele H.*, which Ed told me was based
on the true story of Victor Hugo's daughter, a young woman so
obsessed with a French Army officer that she followed after him
across the sea despite his total indifference, eventually going
stark raving mad, her long dress in tatters and dragging in the
sand. It was the only movie my uncle and I ever saw together
and a very appropriate one too. Yet the funny thing is that as I
watched this story about the tragic dangers of love, of romantic
obsession, it never once entered my mind that my uncle and I,
each unhappily in love with someone we couldn't have, should
be able to relate very personally to this theme and even see it
as warning. But then I was someone capable of taking away from
Lolita and *Swann's Way* that it was relatively normal to become
bewitched by a girl one has very little in common with.

Seeing *The Story of Adele H.* with Uncle Ed actually had a very
buoyant effect on me. As I settled deeper into my plush seat,
my uncle leaned over and whispered that the actor playing the
French Army lieutenant was "so handsome," something I privately disagreed with, since in my opinion the guy seemed gaunt
and a little funny looking. Running through me was a tingling
excitement at being out on the town like this with my uncle,
sitting in this swank theater with its mezzanine and chandeliers,
knowing Laura would be so impressed if she could see me, feeling I was becoming one of this sleek Manhattan audience and
that, with every passing minute, was being improved in some
way so that wonderful things—wonderful new girls—must be in
store for me.

But the feeling didn't stay with me. It wasn't clear for one
thing where I would meet these fabulous new girls. The Tutoring School was almost all boys (after all, to be there you had to
have a royally screwed-up transcript) and after school, riding the
Third Avenue bus back uptown, I'd gaze longingly at girl passengers, particularly the darker-haired ones, since Latinas

seemed to be my type. But there was no avoiding the fact that I was still a nobody who drew no special glances.

The tingling sense of wonderful things to come that I'd felt in the theater had had a lot to do with the feeling of power I got from having my uncle at my side. But on a typical day I saw him around the house only in bits and pieces—in the kitchen, usually, while he puttered around boiling water for tea or preparing a little supper for us. Even then the telephone was always interrupting things. I was aware of the complex life he was trying to juggle—the need to write, to have a million friends, to have nightly sexual adventures, to make a living for himself and me. I'd heard him say how after a few minutes of chatting with any one person he'd begin to feel trapped and want to move on. I'd read the entry in his journal where he'd written: "I am a social animal, most alive, most *myself*, in the crossfire of a hundred eyes, friendly and hostile, at a party." But I still found it very jarring when he cut short even our best chats by standing up suddenly and saying, with a gracious, determined smile, "Okay, kiddo, back to work," or "Okay, kiddo, must fly." And off he'd go back to his old wooden desk in the study with its little green rug and green glass lamp; or out the door to grab a cab.

Sometimes during these little chats with him I could tell he was only half there, going through the motions with me while his mind raced with other things. He'd ask about something I'd already told him about, or tell me something I'd heard him say once or even twice before. Other times I'd feel like a guest on a TV talk show being squeezed for the best of what I had to say in a few minutes of precious airtime. But there were still plenty of times when in the cloudless sunny day of his eyes I could see something so calm and knowing and tuned into me and everyone else and how the whole world worked that to have his attention was almost like being plugged into God. Maybe part of the reason he felt so trapped with any one person was that he was able to put himself so artfully at your disposal that you could never get enough of it and you'd exhaust him. When he was in the right mood he could accommodate me so perfectly that the reason it was so jarring when he abruptly ended our chat was that once again I'd let myself be fooled into thinking I was somehow a special exception to his rule about never lingering in any one conversation for long.

Laura and I were now writing each other every couple days. Her letters would speak whimsically of coming to join me in New York, "if you promise to take care of me and make love to me every night." I'd write back that I was pretty sure we'd be together again someday, though I privately doubted it. It just seemed like she and I were doomed to be kept separate by larger forces. I knew from my study of Stendhal's *Love* that some small amount of hope is needed to keep love alive, that without hope love starved and died like a fire cut off from oxygen. But if this were so then why did I still feel so bad about Laura? What could I possibly be feeling hopeful about? That Uncle Ed would somehow save the day and let Laura come and live with us? Or that I'd find a job (I'd have to leave school) that would support me and Laura in a place of our own?

It didn't help that I was alone so much in the evenings. Knowing that my uncle and Keith McDermott would not be back home till well after I'd gone to bed, I'd turn on the radio and tune in a pop station. Songs that would have made me cringe in embarrassment to hear in front of my uncle now moved me deeply and brought up my rawest feelings about Laura. Not that Uncle Ed was completely above pop music. As a little kid I'd been with him once when the song "Sunny" came on the radio and he'd said that he loved the line "my life was torn like a windblown sail." Only when I was older did I realize he'd misheard—and improved—the line, which actually spoke of windblown *sand*. More recently, I'd heard him say that wasn't it funny how the majority of pop songs were aimed at the very small minority of people who could actually relate to severe, dramatic problems in love. He'd also told me, as though I didn't know it, that many people heard in pop songs all the pathos and stirring spirituality that the rest of us got from serious music.

With my pop songs playing away in the evenings I'd walk through the apartment turning off lights. The place would seem all the more huge in the shadowy half-light, an empty palace where I was a prisoner. Because our apartment sat right above the intersection of Eighty-sixth and Columbus, the city outside was always audible, even in March with the windows closed. Our many tall windows, none of which had shades, also let in the brilliant streetlights, so much more intense than the dim candlepower of the ones in Evanston and so tall that they reached up just short of us on the sixth floor. The windows deepest into the apartment, those in the living room and my uncle's study, looked north across the rooftops of the shorter buildings opposite us on Eighty-sixth Street. This was a noble view full of sky and clouds that inspired lofty thoughts perfectly in keeping with the records my uncle had playing on the record player. But the long western side of the apartment stared at the seedy building of bright orange-red brick opposite us on Columbus Avenue. It fascinated me how our corner stood at the intersection of two such different worlds: Columbus, with its battered storefronts, windblown trash, and shouts from the sidewalk; and Eighty-sixth Street, which just east of us became a stately canyon of tall apartment buildings where uniformed doormen helped fur-coated ladies out to the curb under canopied entrances.

The worlds I could see inside the apartment windows were so different too. On the Columbus side, Puerto Rican men in sleeveless Italian T-shirts paced around throwing sharp shadows under bare, high-watt lightbulbs. But on the Eighty-sixth Street side pianos gleamed discreetly through a scrim of potted plants and I saw more dogs than people—small, expensive purebred dogs waiting to be walked the long tree-lined block over to Central Park. Rainy nights, I'd stand watching the shiny yellow taxis streaming south down Columbus through the intersection smeared with the long, candy-colored reflections of traffic lights. As the bright rainwater threaded down the sewer drain, I'd fantasize about breaking Laura out of the convent, scaling its high stone wall, and carrying her off in the dead of night. Where would we go? Perhaps we'd live in the fort, or in a dugout in the bank of the canal.

I couldn't think of Laura without thinking about sex and soon I'd be jerking off in the little water closet (just a toilet, nothing else) attached to my maid's room. My uncle and Keith McDermott kept a bunch of amyl nitrite—poppers—in the freezer, and since I'd heard them rave about how it prolonged your orgasm if you sniffed some just as you were about to come, I decided to give it a try. But it was a complete failure. As soon as I inhaled the stuff, all the blood in my dick went flooding up to my head.

But then one day a dramatic letter came from Laura. She said she'd been nearly six months pregnant, and that the baby was definitely ours, since of course she hadn't slept with anybody else since she'd met me. What must have happened is that she'd forgotten to take some of her birth control pills last fall when we were in the fort all the time. Anyway, the baby, our baby, was dead. She didn't want to go into it now but it was her stupid father who'd made her lose it—"loose" it, as she wrote. There was so much to tell me about when she saw me again. But for now I should know that she was in Indiana. It was a long story but things were getting real bad at the convent and she had to make a run for it. She was okay—scared but okay. She had to keep her address secret even from me till things settled down. I should pray for her. She'd write again soon.

That evening the phone rang and it was a collect call from Laura. There'd been something fishy about her letter (it was postmarked CHICAGO, for one thing) and, sure enough, Laura admitted she was "just being dramatic" about leaving the convent and, yeah, about being pregnant and losing the baby too. But she really did need to get the hell out of the convent. And real soon too. "There's something funny going on here," she said. "They feel this is not the right place for me. They want me to see another psychiatrist and even asked me if I would like to go back to McNeal or to St. Joseph's Hospital. But no way I'm gonna go back to the funny farm. I got all angry with the nuns about it and threatened everybody, so now Sister Dominic is in the process of trying to send me to that horrible correctional place for girls in Geneva."

Laura said she'd become friends at the convent with a girl called Christie who knew some people in Gary, Indiana, willing to let her and Laura come live with them. Laura thought this plan sounded better than her other plan of splitting to Mexico by herself because Christie told her that once Laura crossed over into Mexico it would be almost impossible ever to return to the States.

After I signed off with Laura, I immediately called my mother and told her I wanted to come to Chicago for a visit with her. Next week was spring break and I could take the train. My mother got all excited and said she'd wire me the money for the train tickets. Then I called up my friend Bryan in Evanston and as we talked we found ourselves saying that maybe we could break Laura out of the convent—maybe the three of us could even all live together in an apartment of our own in New York. It was fun to talk about doing such bold, daring things.

In Penn Station I got on board the Broadway Limited and a full twenty-four hours later the train pulled into Chicago's Union Station. Feeling like a zombie from sitting up all night, I joined the slow river of people making their way up the cold, concrete platform. Someone jostled my shoulder much more roughly than necessary just as I passed through the blast of heated air at the entrance to the concourse. When I turned around it was Laura.

I'd forgotten how much healthier she looked than most people, the hair and eyes shinier, the skin not sickly pale. Giggling with delight at my shock, she said, "What's the matter—don't remember me?" And then: "So aren't you even going to kiss me?"

She'd never looked sexier: her mane of hair was wilder and longer than ever, falling well past her shoulders now, and she'd lost a few more pounds of baby fat. When I kissed her there was that smell again of hers that I'd forgotten how much I loved, Jōvan Musk. Strangely, she didn't have a word to say about my greatly improved skin. But then she was so much more hyperactive than I'd remembered, jiggling around with the hectic energy of a puppy dog, her sparkling brown eyes refusing to focus on anything but her own silly merriment.

Outside the station a raw wind whipped our hair in all directions and I remembered my uncle saying that even the weather in Chicago was uncivilized—that "sable is the only solution" for such a bitterly cold climate. As Laura and I were crossing broad La Salle Street against the light, some oncoming cars sent me jogging for the safety of the far curb but Laura, I noticed, continued walking serenely along, head held high, as though she couldn't be bothered with the cars screeching to a halt around her. It came back to me that it was some kind of point of honor with her never to have to run, which she considered beneath her dignity.

"So did you run away from the convent?" I asked her.

"What do you think?"

"Are you still going to Indiana?"

"Are you still going back to New York?"

It felt so unreal to be back with Laura, to be back in Chicago. In the Jackson Street subway station I had to smile as the little green and white El train came pulling in. Compared to the graffiti-streaked monsters of the New York subways, the El looked laughably toylike. "So how did you get away?" I asked Laura.

"Shhh, I can't tell you till we get inside someplace."

"So should we go to my mother's place?"

"Is she there?"

"No, she's at work."

My mother had left the key under the doormat. Because she and Phyl wouldn't be home from their social worker jobs for hours, I saw no problem in making love with Laura on their four-poster bed. It had been so long since we'd fucked—five months?—that it was all deliciously new again. But the truly new thing we did together was take a hot bath afterward. The bathtub in my mother's bathroom was a big, queen-sized thing and being naked with Laura in it under the bright overhead light was far more revealing than any of our burrowing sex had been. Now, as she showed me how she liked to soap up a sponge and scrub every inch of herself with what seemed to me absurd thoroughness, I could really see how perfect she was.

Laura said she and her friend Christie had escaped two or three days ago, it was hard to keep track of the time. They'd run away during a field trip. Because it was a cold day, Sister Dominic had allowed them to wear long pants under their pleated navy blue convent skirts and when Laura and Christie suddenly bolted away from the group, they threw their skirts into a garbage dumpster in an alley they'd gone running up. "Christie's not too pleased that I'm with you today, to tell you the truth," Laura said. She was leaning over me now, suds dripping off her breasts, not satisfied with the cleaning job I'd done on myself and taking her sponge to me with a mother's irritating avidity. As she worked away on me, she bit on her upper lip and peeped out her tongue in adorable concentration. "Actually, Christie freaked out this morning when I told her I was going to meet you. She probably thinks you might try to steal me away from her, I guess."

"But why? I mean, why should she care?"

"Well, Christie's a pretty needy person. She's nice and everything but she's also real intense and kind of possessive, you know?"

Just after Laura climbed out of the tub, pretty body dripping, and went over to the mirror to brush out her hair because, as she explained, her hair was so damn thick and curly that only when it was wet could she even pull a brush through it, I heard the muffled, excited voice of the only person in world who calls me "Keithie." It was my mother. Jesus. She'd come home early.

Though they certainly knew about each other, my mother and Laura had never actually met. My mother was normally a big hugger, someone who got ecstatic at reunions of any kind. But today she'd come home to find her and Phyl's bed all messed up from our lovemaking and our clothes, our underwear, scattered all over their bedroom floor. With a face that looked hard and exhausted, my mother told Laura, "Honey, I'm sorry, but I'm going to have to ask you to leave. What you do in your life is none of my business, but *my* life is. And this is my apartment."

As I walked Laura to the El station, she asked me if I thought my mother was going to call the cops on her. I told her no, but Laura, still smarting from the confrontation, muttered, "What a bitch." Then she did an exaggerated imitation of the way Mom's chin jutted out because of her severe underbite. "This is my life, Keithie, goddamnit!" she mimicked. "My life!"

"So where have you and Christie been staying?" I asked. "In Indiana?"

"Well, to be honest with you, Christie and I got thrown out of there. Now we got this new plan to go to Scottsdale, Arizona. Christie's got some kind of relative out there."

"But where are you guys staying now?"

"Oh, you know, around."

"Around" turned out to be Lyons, Illinois, a western suburb next door to Berwyn and our dear McNeal Hospital. Lyons was Christie's old stomping ground, apparently.

Laura didn't have a phone where she could be reached, so at the Sheridan El station we decided that she would call me in the morning at my mother's place after Mom had gone to work. Geographically, Laura and I could not have kissed each other good-bye in a place closer to the center of the forces at work in our lives. Just a few blocks to the south and west, at the foot of the enormous Graceland Cemetery, stood the House of the Good Shepherd. Five blocks to the east, in the narrow band of middle-class affluence hugging the lake, was my mother's place.

The area surrounding us here at Sheridan Station, meanwhile, was a poor Hispanic neighborhood of currency exchanges and *grocerias* draped in protective metal grates and still twinkling with delirious Christmas lights.

When Laura had gone I literally began walking back toward the middle class—back toward the luxury high-rises, with their expensive little food "commissaries" off the lobby, and the brick apartment buildings like my mother's with their deep, tidy courtyards. The closer I got to the lake, the farther I felt from Laura.

I was sure my mother was waiting for me with a long speech about how I shouldn't let Laura run—and ruin—my life. That with all I'd been through and all that had gone into freeing me and getting me back on my feet again, I would be a fool to let Laura bring everything tumbling down again. That calls were going to be made to Uncle Ed, to the convent, to Laura's parents. That, goddamnit, she hadn't paid for my train tickets just so I could shack up with a runaway girl in her apartment. Instead, my mother gave me a big hug when I came in the door. She told me that my life was mine to live but did I really see any future with someone who always seemed surrounded by so much trouble? And that was it. For the rest of my visit the subject never came up again. I guess the one thing Mom and I had learned from our old screaming fights was to treat each other as carefully as explosives.

That evening I sat on the living room couch that I'd been given for a bed and, with the door closed, called up my friend Bryan. Sounding intrigued by Laura's friend Christie, Bryan helped me come up with the idea of meeting up with Laura and Christie the next night at the Spot, the Evanston pizza restaurant where I'd performed so many times. The Spot would be easy for everybody to get to, being right next to an El station. But the next night it began to look like Laura and Christie weren't going to show up. Laura had sounded all for the idea earlier that day on the phone, and since talking to her I'd even managed to find a place where we could all hang out and spend the night.

When Bryan said his house was no good because he could never be certain that his mother would be spending the night at her boyfriend's place, I went to see my friend Donny—the friend who'd gone to visit Uncle Ed with me back in 1973 and given my uncle's chicken hawk friend the best day of his life. Donny was now living in a huge house in South Evanston with his father and stepmother. He said he had the whole top floor of the house to himself and that we could party up there all night if we wanted because his father and stepmother couldn't hear anything from their own floor.

But now it was nearly midnight and the Spot was about to close. Donny, Bryan, and I had been sitting for hours at a large round table with two empty chairs, watching the doorway. When we'd first walked in I'd been surprised by how comically suburban this old hangout of mine seemed with its exposed brick walls, hanging ferns, and friendly, nasal-accented waitresses. My old music mentor, the mustachioed M.C. who'd thought about adopting me the year before, came over to say hello but failed to exclaim anything like the "Hey, you look terrific!" that Donny's father had when he caught sight of my cleared-up skin and New York hair. Instead, the Spot M.C. glanced at the jean jacket and blue Italian shirt I was wearing and said with a smirk, "Oh, so this is what they're wearing in New York now." When he found out I'd let my music lapse completely since going to live with my uncle, he grew even more cold and remote.

When the Spot closed, Donny, Bryan, and I stood out in the gravel parking lot next to the Foster El station, smoking cigarettes and singing "Tim Finnegan's Wake." The Evanston El trains were few and far between this time of night but two or three of them had come and gone when finally, as the latest little single-car El went clattering off into the distance, we heard raised female voices echoing in the stairwell of the station. It was Laura and Christie at last. "Christie has to get high," a disgusted-sounding Laura announced to us. "So I'm supposed to ask you guys if you know some place where we can go score something." Donny said he had some dope in his bong at home and, since that's where we'd planned on going anyway, we all climbed into Bryan's car and drove over there.

In the dark I hadn't gotten a very good look at Christie. But at Donny's house I saw that she was a very pale girl with bleached blonde hair wearing a pair of pale old jeans so tight they seemed molded to her skinny flanks. She had the kind of green eyes I instinctively didn't trust; shifty, fishy-looking eyes. Though I'd wanted to be nice to her and maybe win her over a bit, I immediately felt a negatively charged atmosphere between us. She was a couple years older than Laura—about my age, I think—and something Laura had said about her popped into my mind: "Christie's the instigator of everything we do." Because she certainly was turning out to be bossy. As we all sat around taking long, bubbling tokes from the bong, Christie got up and ejected from the tape player the music that Donny, our host, had put on, replacing it with a tape of Elton John's *Goodbye Yellow Brick Road* that she'd fished out of her bag. "Gotta hear my music!" she shouted, cranking up the volume. *Goodbye Yellow Brick Road* was apparently the only music she'd consent to listen to.

When we were all high, Laura and I left the room and went off to a spare bedroom down the hall to have sex. I'd had the fleeting thought that Donny or Bryan might hit it off with Christie but a few minutes later a restless Christie was banging on the door, telling Laura that she was bored, so bored she'd decided to go back to Indiana for a day or two. It seemed she'd already directed Donny to roll her a nice joint for the road and enlisted poor Bryan into driving her there.

The rest of my spring vacation in Chicago is mostly just a big blur now—in memory it's all become one long night, though it must have been two or three. Did Laura more or less move into the top floor of Donny's house? Did I? If so, how did I ever swing all this with my mother? One thing I do remember is that not long after Bryan and Christie had driven off in the night for Indiana, Laura fell dead asleep right in the middle of talking with me and Donny, the lights and music around her all up high—suffering, I guess, from that total exhaustion that hits fugitives when they've pulled themselves into a safe hole after days on the run.

I remember staring at Laura and feeling that wonder you feel at the mystery of the sleeping person. Had this person ever really been mine? This slender, breathing body, sleeping on its side in the jeans now too big at the waist and cinched in with a big leather belt? These bent legs in their little white socks? This thick, tumbling head of hair resting on a smooth young arm in its T-shirt? As I watched her sleep a hundred sad, helpless thoughts flooded through my mind. Already, I felt the gulf opening up between us again. Now, this moment, she was here in my life but it would all be over so soon. Having hooked up with Christie, Laura would be off to Arizona before long where I'd probably never see her again.

I remember Bryan returning at some point to tell us that Christie hadn't uttered a word throughout the long drive to Indiana, contenting herself with smoking and listening to her *Yellow Brick Road* over and over. But just when and how Christie rejoined us escapes me now. Perhaps Bryan had to drive out to Indiana again to fetch her. All I know is that by the time I staggered back on board my Broadway Limited train, I felt like someone coming down from a massive acid trip—the kind of trip that leaves you drained yet still racing from overstimulation, the morning sun shining with painful sharpness into your eyes. I remember breathing in the smell of diesel fumes as I stood in a vestibule in between train cars, the metal plates shifting beneath my feet as we rocked and switched tracks, slowly departing Chicago through a tangle of freight yard tracks. Running through my mind over and over was the last song on *Yellow Brick Road*, "Harmony," whose opening bars, with their wearily beautiful minor chords, captured the aching, enchanted sense of doom inside me. "Hello, baby, hello . . . haven't seen your face for a while . . . have you quit doin' time for me . . . ?"

For the second time this new year I was leaving Chicago and Laura behind.

PHOTO BY KEITH McDERMOTT

Playing house

It was natural to view everything with literary eyes in my uncle's apartment and back in New York I suddenly saw everything in terms of the novel *Manon Lescaut*. Uncle Ed told me I might find *Manon* interesting reading; boy, he got that right. As I began turning the pages of this eighteenth-century love story, the parallels to me and Laura kept leaping out at me. The beautiful Manon is being sent by coach to a convent as punishment for her incorrigible "inclination to pleasure." But on the way there she happens to meet our seventeen-year-old hero who instantly decides to help her escape. Together they flee to the capital where they live together in a small apartment. Though she's a couple years younger than he, she's the one who's experienced in love. She's worldly and full of fun, while he's shy and uptight. She's the first girlfriend he's ever had. He's so swept off his feet by her that he devotes himself completely to her, the future be damned. But then his father tracks him down and has him locked up. A few months go by and the boy is given a second chance to make good with his life. He applies himself diligently to his studies, making every effort to forget his bewitching girlfriend. But one day Manon shows up unexpectedly and he falls for her all over again. This time it's for good and brings his ruin, for the novel makes clear that the boy has always had only two options: a drab life of solitary virtue or an out-of-control life of sin with Manon.

Laura had begun calling me collect at my uncle's every couple days. She'd always purr, "Hi, Keith," in her lowest, most insinuating voice and then wait for me to guess it was she. I could just picture her eyes narrowing dreamily as her eyebrows arched flirtatiously. Though she and Christie were still planning to go to Arizona, Laura said that maybe they'd come and see me in New York first. But first Laura was writing a letter to Sister Dominic:

> Dear Sister Dominic,
> It hasn't been even two weeks since I escaped from your wonderful setting. I hope that you don't miss me as much as I do, because I don't miss you at all. I think I am a nice kid to be forgotten just like that, don't you agree?
> To be as truthful and honest as I can I feel miserable. I haven't been "straight" this whole time, but in some ways I feel alright. This way I don't think about any problems and trash like that . . .

I asked Laura if she was really getting high all the time and she said, "No—well, yeah, pretty much." I asked what kind of drugs she was doing and she said, "Oh, just some THC and a lot of speed. Christie's really into speed."

"But where do you get these drugs?"

"Well," Laura said, "there's this bar here where Christie knows people."

"I mean, where do you get the money for it?"

"Well, we usually don't pay."

"Oh," I said.

Laura said I shouldn't worry; I should trust her. Usually the guys who gave them drugs were older guys who felt kind of sorry for them. They were like older brothers, especially to Laura, since she was still such a kid, only fourteen.

I'd learned it never did much good to talk to my uncle about jealousy. According to him, jealousy had nothing to do with sex. "What makes us jealous is not our loved one having sex with someone else," he'd explained to me, "but rather the thought that he or she might *care* for this other person more than they do us." Since Laura was calling me constantly and obviously cared about me, I felt I couldn't talk about my jealousy to Uncle Ed; by his lights I had no right to be jealous.

But I was sleeping worse than ever on my little single bed in the maid's room. I'd lie there listening to the sirens out in the night. When I'd first moved in my uncle said I'd soon grow so used to New York street noise that I'd no longer notice it, but my maid's room was by far the noisiest bedroom in the apartment, the only one on the street side (Ed's and Keith's bedrooms were both over on the quiet courtyard side). Lying in bed I'd feel the world quaking at its foundations as the trucks rumbling down Columbus Avenue jolted into potholes. On rainy nights the river of late-night traffic sounded like bacon sizzling on a busy grill. When I just couldn't sleep I'd stare at the dingy brown-yellow window shade I kept permanently drawn against the strong streetlight, trying not to get too frantic about the possibility that Laura might be screwing some of these guys who'd been giving them drugs and a place to stay. Her actually fucking someone else was an image too terrible for my mind to picture.

I hadn't breathed a word to my uncle about Laura lately. I didn't want to burden him with any more of my problems, nor did I want him to know that it had even crossed my mind to drop out, get a job and an apartment, and throw away all he'd done to get me back on track. But then one day the impossible happened. It seemed that what I was feeling had all been transparent to him. He'd noticed the big change in me since I'd come back from Chicago, the way I was sleeping even worse than usual, jumping to my feet whenever the phone rang. And when I told him that Laura had run away from the convent and was now on the loose in Chicago, he said, as though it were the simplest thing in the world, "Well, since it seems you can't live without her, I guess she could come live with you here."

This fresh proof of how unlike anybody else in the world he was reminded me that at times like this just hearing his voice could give me the feeling that anything, magical things, had become possible; that for all I knew his kind, casual voice might keep right on going and tell me he'd arranged it for me to be famous and live forever.

But Laura and I would not be able to live with him here at the apartment. "There's something called the Mann Law," he explained, "which makes it a crime for an adult like me to harbor a minor like Laura under my roof for even a single night." Given this, he suggested I start looking into rooms for rent in the area—that way we could all have some meals together at least.

But when I told Laura the great news, she said she needed time to make up her mind. She felt responsible for poor Christie now, you see. And since I wouldn't let Christie come to New York too, Laura worried Christie might freak out if she were suddenly deserted.

As bad as it had been to have the adult world keeping me and Laura apart, it was a new kind of torture to have Laura's own ambivalence be what stood in our way. I did my best to weather with stoic dignity the terrible suspense of waiting for her answer over the next few days. I tried not to talk too much about it to my uncle, having heard him say once that "nothing is more boring than having to listen to someone else's problems in love."

But the next time Laura called, I couldn't believe what she had to say. As I wrote to my friend Bryan:

> It seems she and dear Christie hitched a ride with a truck driver who drove them all over the country. They are now stranded in Atlanta, Georgia. I try not to think (worry) about Laura. It's not good for my health.

It was Uncle Ed who'd warned me to look after my health. He said he'd never seen someone suffer so much, that even the balled-up sheets on my bed had a look of shockingly intense grief. Yet all attempts to control myself were useless. In some horrible way it was fitting, I guess, that Laura should end up stuck in Georgia, since it dramatized even on a geographic level how torn she felt between a future with me in New York and one with Christie in Arizona.

One haggard morning the phone rang while my uncle and I were eating breakfast. He took the call and his eyes immediately met mine with a look that let me know it was Laura, who'd never called so early before. Accepting the charges, he handed me the phone and told me, "She's in *Texas* now." Laura, sounding very small and a bit sniffly, said she'd just escaped from Christie but was afraid Christie would come after her when she woke up.

Hearing that Laura was scared and asking for help, Uncle Ed decided on the spot that we had to get Laura out of there by flying her to New York. But there was a totally unexpected hitch: it seemed Laura had never been in an airport, much less an airplane. No matter how we tried to convince her that she could manage by herself to get to the airport, pick up the ticket Ed would wire there, and board the plane, she kept saying she didn't think she could do it. In the end my uncle decided there was nothing to do but fly *me* down to fetch her. He also came up with the idea that Laura should wait for me in downtown Fort Worth on the steps of the city hall.

Just hours after talking to Laura, I landed at the Dallas/Fort Worth airport. My uncle had lent me a sport coat and tie because "It's important that you look respectable. Texans feel almost more racist about Mexicans than they do blacks." This information only heightened the drama of my mission. Having been given more than a hundred dollars for what Uncle Ed said would be a long, expensive cab ride to Fort Worth, I had plenty of time to sit there stewing as the taxi sped along past sunbaked pastures, the highway asphalt shimmering in the intense heat. Had Laura been able to find city hall? More important, did she have the patience to wait for me there all this time? And what about Christie? Could Laura have been recaptured by her? Or picked up by the police?

Miraculously, Laura was there, waiting faithfully on the wide, shallow marble stairs. She'd become so skinny that her jeans looked strangely huge and droopy on her. I jumped out of the taxi to embrace her, finding it hard to believe that here, under this alien sun, our troubles had finally come to an end and that after six months of obstacles and separations Laura was finally mine.

All the way back to New York, Laura filled me in on the events leading up to her big break with Christie. These big old jeans she was wearing weren't even hers. You see, these two dumb guys who lived in Fort Worth had picked her and Christie up on the highway and invited them to spend the night at their house. Right away, Christie went upstairs to screw one of them, leaving Laura in the living room with the other guy, the one with the broken leg. He told Laura he had some great microdot acid for them to trip on. Except it turned out this dumb guy had accidentally dropped the acid into the shag carpet weeks ago and now they needed to get down on their knees and try to find the stuff. They spent hours combing through every inch of his stupid carpet but never found the fuckers. Finally, the guy fell asleep in an armchair. It was like eight in the morning by now and Christie and the other guy were still upstairs, sleeping.

This was her big chance, Laura realized. You see, in the past few days Christie had been getting more and more jealous and worried about Laura deciding in the end to go to me. Christie hated for Laura to even hear the words *New York*, and on the way to Georgia with the truck driver Christie got all upset when the national weather report came on the radio and they mentioned New York. Later, Laura made the mistake of talking about me and Christie got drunk and started berating Laura. It was scary how angry she got. Laura said to herself, "This is it." And so, with everyone in the house asleep that morning, Laura helped herself to a clean pair of jeans from the broken-leg guy's dresser drawers and went running out into the morning, calling me and Uncle Ed from the first pay phone she came to.

Several times Laura told me how nervous she was about meeting my uncle; she was afraid he wouldn't like her. But he liked Laura right away, telling me later that she reminded him of a lioness with her mane of hair, which had grown very wild during her weeks on the run, falling into her face so that you could hardly see her eyes. "Hiding behind her hair," he said. He also noticed she had a nervous habit of tapping her shoe on the floor. Through my uncle's eyes, in fact, I was appreciating aspects to Laura I hadn't been conscious of before he pointed them out— that she had a low voice, for instance, and that her hips were slender, like a boy's. But the weirdest thing my uncle told me was that when he was my age he'd been "madly in love" with a girl sort of like Laura—a girl with the same slender hips and big breasts. He'd sent this girl a declaration of love he wrote on special parchment paper because he felt that if only she would become his girlfriend, he'd be able to put behind him for good the homosexual impulses that had been plaguing him since puberty. When her polite rejection arrived in the mail, he'd felt doomed to a "homosexual fate." But then "that was back in the desperate fifties, when being gay felt like the end of the world," he said with a laugh.

I'd found a cheap room for me and Laura right across the street. It was in the same seedy orange-red brick building full of men pacing in Italian T-shirts that I'd stared out at during those rainy nights alone in my uncle's apartment. The whole building reeked of sickly sweet roach spray and the walls of our little room felt as flimsy and porous as the walls of the backyard fort in Evanston. Deep in the night I'd wake up to coughs and Spanish voices and think for a moment they belonged to people who'd somehow gotten into our room. In the morning I'd head off for school, the smell of roach spray clinging to my clothes.

Fortunately, our close proximity to Uncle Ed's meant that our little room was more like an outpost—more like a distant, shabby corner of my uncle's apartment where Laura and I would head off to sleep each night. We ate most of our dinners with my uncle because our place had no kitchen; and I continued to stink up his bathroom every night with my sulfur acne treatment because there was no way to boil water at our place and the only bathroom was a cruddy, communal one down the hall. During the day, while I was off at the Tutoring School, Laura spent hours over at Uncle Ed's. He'd hired her at a generous wage to clean his apartment, though he usually pitched in and helped her. The two of them sometimes got so silly while they were cleaning together, he told me, that they pranced around with chairs held upside down on top of their heads as they prepared to mop the kitchen floor.

Cleaning would give way to English lessons conducted at the kitchen table. Because it had been only two years since Laura and her family had immigrated from Mexico, her English was still peppered with idioms she translated directly from Spanish (my favorite being *assist in* a concert instead of attend one). But Laura told me she'd never felt self-conscious about being Mexican in an Anglo world. It was my uncle, in fact, who kept drawing her attention to it, telling her things like, "You have such great naturally tanned skin. If you went to Germany everyone would love you there." Soon Uncle Ed had succeeded in convincing her that "it's actually an asset to be darker."

Because my uncle always had his writing to do, a big part of Laura's English lessons became the reading he assigned her. Just as I had done, Laura would lie on the living room sofa reading, though the books she read were *The Catcher in the Rye* and *Last Exit to Brooklyn*. My uncle's ceaseless energy amused her—"the way he keeps running back and forth in the apartment," making more tea or coffee or answering the constantly ringing phone at different ends of the apartment. It particularly amused her to see him typing in his study while talking on the phone at the same time. One day Laura overheard him consulting his lawyer on the phone about the possibility of legally adopting her. Though my uncle learned that this was out of the question, he'd nonetheless come to feel more and more like a parent to both Laura and me—so much so that he'd started telling people at parties that he had a teenage son and daughter.

Hanging out at the apartment, Laura also saw something of Keith McDermott, whose nocturnal *Equus* and social schedule left him free only during the day for a few hours. If Keith referred to himself as "Mom" around me, around Laura he became "your great-aunt." Laura thought it was cool the way Keith lounged around the house in white painters' pants, drinking from a Perrier bottle filled with chilled tap water. Sometimes he'd unwind by lumbering into the kitchen pretending to be a zombie. But the coolest thing Keith did was give Laura and me complimentary tickets—"comps," as he called them—for a special matinee performance of *Equus*. This was the day that Richard Burton, officially scheduled to replace Tony Perkins only the following week, would make his surprise debut. As the lights went down Laura and I smiled knowingly while the rest of the audience groaned at the announcement that Anthony Perkins would not be appearing in the role of Dr. Martin Dysart today. Giving no hint that anyone but an anonymous understudy would be performing in Perkins' place, the announcement continued: "Replacing him in the role today, Richard Burton." The ecstatic applause that erupted lasted several minutes.

Our front row seats were not the usual ones. In a trendy touch, bleachers had been set up on the edge of the stage itself so that Laura and I sat there within spitting distance of the actors. And Richard Burton, I think, must have felt like spitting on us. For when the lights came up on the famous actor, Laura blurted out to me, "God, he's so old," in a voice that Keith McDermott later said carried very clearly to him, several feet downstage from Burton.

Keith had a theory that fans like Laura were so accustomed to seeing celebrities on-screen that when they encountered them in the flesh, the celebrity didn't quite seem real to them. It was as though fans believed their comments couldn't be heard by the stars. The only movie Laura had seen Burton in was *Cleopatra*, and so even though she'd heard Uncle Ed say that Burton's heavy drinking had put such hard mileage on his handsome face that "all that's left, really, is that wonderful, rich voice—so big it rattles the floorboards," it still shocked Laura to see Burton looking so much craggier than his early sixties *Cleopatra* self.

What I myself found most shocking about *Equus* was the character of the psychiatrist. For "Dr. Dysart" couldn't be more utterly different from Dr. Schwarz. Dysart is reluctant to take on new patients, for one thing, worrying he already has too many. And when he does agree to work with troubled young Alan Strang, he treats this belligerent, nutty boy (who's just blinded six horses) with endless patience and indulgence. Schwarz, I kept thinking, would have sent the kid straight to the "quiet room" where he would have been tied down to the bed until he cut the crap. Dysart is also haunted by fits of conscience and doubt, the feeling that he's working in the dark with his patients and might in his ignorance actually be harming them. By play's end, when he's cured the boy of his madness, Dysart fears he's robbed the boy of his magic, his passion, and replaced it with a banal normality. But then of course this notion of a romantic, poetic madness, as I'd learned from my uncle, was itself banal.

To help pay for Laura's and my rented room, I'd taken an after-school job at a midtown Merrill Lynch office where I stuffed envelopes for the mass mailings a gay stockbroker friend of my uncle's was continually sending out to potential clients. One evening after work I came straight to my uncle's apartment because Laura and I had the place to ourselves that night. Uncle Ed had gone up to Yale University for the day and wouldn't be back till very late. When Laura greeted me by serving up cold glasses of some cherry Kool-Aid she'd prepared, I thought it seemed a little odd but I wrote it off to her making a game of playing house. A few minutes later Laura asked me slyly, "Feeling just a little bit weird, Keith?" As soon as she said this, I did feel a bit weird. Weirder and weirder, in fact. "You haven't taken a hit of acid or anything recently, have you?" she asked. When I told her no, she said with a slowly growing smile, "Are you sure?"

When it came out that she'd spiked the Kool-Aid with LSD bought from a guy on Columbus Avenue, I got angry at first. But then I decided there was nothing to be done but go with the thing. Soon Laura and I had wandered out into the tiled hallway outside my uncle's apartment where a flight of marble stairs leading up to the roof attracted our attention. These stairs were unlit and off limits but as Laura's electric Kool-Aid really began to kick in we decided to mount them, giggling in the dusty, deepening darkness and pushing open a heavy, stubborn door at the top. A fairy-tale vision sprang up all around us: in every direction, like castle turrets peeping above the treetops in a forest, little black water towers rose up from the surrounding rooftops. I completely forgot about Laura. Only when she called out that she was going to jump off the building did I notice she'd climbed up onto the narrow stone ledge at the edge of the roof. Too terrified of heights to do anything but stand a few feet away from her, imploring her for what felt like hours not to jump, I remember resenting the devil-may-care way she kept laughing and mocking me by saying, "Why are you getting all worried?"

What a relief when she finally tired of her stunt because she thought she'd left her cigarettes in the kitchen. And how wonderful to leave the outside world and all its dangers and return to my uncle's apartment, which enveloped us like a fortress, one that was our universe and that belonged to us.

Over the next few hours, as we played records and horsed around, Laura and I managed to wreck the stylus on my uncle's record player. By the time he came home the whole place was in some disarray. "Oh, I see," my tired uncle said when we told him about the broken record needle. His exasperation was pitched so subtly that I wondered if Laura could hear it. My uncle's diplomacy was so much a part of him that the few times he'd ever said anything pointed to me became memorable events. There'd been the whimsical moment I'd told him I was thinking of maybe becoming a cowboy when he'd startled me by acting genuinely alarmed and disapproving: "Oh, now what would be the point of that?" Or the time I'd heard him mutter "pearls before swine" when I'd failed to show much excitement about the difficult Stravinsky piece he'd just played for me on the record player. I'd never seen my uncle lose his temper but tonight I could see in his taut face a barely perceptible boil within him. Laura, however, was gaily telling him that she felt so wrecked she didn't think she'd be able to make it back across the street to our room—could she crash here tonight? In a haze of embarrassment, I apologized to my uncle and headed out the door. When Laura didn't follow after me, I went back to our rented room by myself.

The next day Laura told me all about the eventful night she'd spent at Uncle Ed's. He'd said she could crash in my old maid's room but Laura, still speeding from the acid, found it impossible to sleep. Roaming through the apartment, she went to the bathroom, and then, on impulse, entered Ed's bedroom and crawled under the covers with him. Laura sensed as she settled in beside him that he was only pretending to be asleep and that it had "kind of shocked" him that she'd gotten into bed with him like this. Whatever he was doing, he eventually turned over toward her and Laura told him, "I just want to sleep here 'cause I'm afraid." He took her in his arms and they kissed, but then he seemed to decide that what they were doing was wrong because he suddenly told her, "You need to go to sleep. Here, I'm going to give you a Valium. That'll make you sleepy."

The upshot of the whole experience was that Laura came away feeling Uncle Ed was the only person she'd met who didn't want to take advantage of her in some fashion, who truly cared about her in a pure, disinterested way. She coined a pet name for him: "Teddy," as in teddy bear. And yet, interestingly, Laura didn't believe her Teddy to be completely innocent of sexual interest in her. No, she thought it was more a matter of his willpower, of his deciding to be a gentleman, a father to her.

My uncle was too sensitive to my feelings to say anything to me at the time but years later he told me that one night when he'd taken me and Laura to Twelve West, a big gay discotheque in an old warehouse, Laura had confided to him that if she cared to, she was certain that many of the handsome gay men dancing around them could be tempted into having sex with her. My uncle concluded that Laura was such a sexual being, and so accustomed to being sexually desirable to men, that it was inconceivable to her that any man, even a gay one, could resist her. (I, on the other hand, had such "faith" in my uncle's homosexuality that it never occurred to me to be jealous of Laura's night in bed with him.)

Still, I was *somewhat* aware then that Laura could see things in very sexual terms. I knew, for instance, that she'd suspected Christie of "having the hots" for her just because Laura couldn't imagine any other reason for Christie's intense possessiveness. And the first thing Laura asked me after meeting Uncle Ed was whether he'd tried to get in my pants. I'd told her no because telling her the truth would have involved too much explaining.

I would have needed her to see my uncle's little spur-of-the-moment come-on to me against the backdrop of randy, mid-1970s Manhattan—a milieu where one could enter an apartment building, as I did the day I rented Laura's and my room, and see through an open door the young super, dressed only in underpants, lying on a bed in his studio apartment and beckoning one to join him. Another time, I'd been standing at a red light at Broadway and Eighty-sixth when a twenty-something couple approached me and asked if I had a light. Then they asked if I wanted to come home with them. The woman looked pretty good but I couldn't see myself doing anything with the guy. And yet after I'd shyly told them no, I watched them hurry away and thought to myself: I've just passed up an offer that comes once in a lifetime. (I was right.)

My uncle told me he was concerned sometimes that Laura might be getting the wrong idea from the example he was setting—"She must find it confusing how my friends and I always seem to be just having fun, when the truth is that we're also holding down jobs, paying bills, not letting things get *too* out of hand." Keeping things in proportion amid so many temptations, he said, required a special kind of discipline that was hard to see, let alone teach. But there were no more incidents like the electric Kool-Aid night and soon it was June. Uncle Ed was asked to give a speech at my Tutoring School on the last day of school. I can't remember what the speech was about, only that he'd spent several hours preparing and typing it up, and that when he delivered it to the school's small student body and faculty I could feel how everyone admired him. It was the kind of proud public moment I'd never experienced with my real father.

Uncle Ed had been asked to speak at the school by my English teacher, Mr. Manchester, an intriguing man in his fifties with a proud mane of hair the color of old teeth. After meeting him, my uncle speculated that Mr. Manchester was "an old-fashioned closeted gay man who must have suffered some terrible tragedy in his life," which would explain how someone so talented and sophisticated could be ending his days teaching at the Tutoring School. Whatever his story, Mr. Manchester was my favorite teacher and I'd blossomed under his sharp eye and his way of conducting class with a cheerful mock exasperation that made me feel I'd become a delightfully cheeky wag. "That's quite enough from you, Mr. Fleming," he'd tell me, the faintest smile betraying his affection. It was for him that I'd written the essay on love in which I'd found Erich Fromm so inferior in wisdom to Stendhal.

What a shame that my final moment with Mr. Manchester was so strange and disturbing. With my uncle standing nearby chatting with my strapping young science teacher, and classmates milling around us, telling one another to "Have a nice life," I was saying good-bye to Mr. Manchester when I must have said something about my uncle that Mr. Manchester misheard. "What's that?" he asked. "You say your uncle is after you?"

It was such an embarrassing moment that I can't remember what, if anything, I replied. Perhaps I just cringed and mumbled something as I turned away.

That summer my uncle found me and Laura a studio apartment on West Fifteenth Street. It amused us to hear it was called a "garden apartment" just because it happened to be on the ground floor, in the back, and looked out on a sunless, ivied courtyard we had no access to. But after life in the sweet stink of the roach-sprayed rented room it was great to have a real place of our own. Our new bathroom was still down the hall, with an antique toilet you flushed by pulling a chain attached to the water tank overhead, but it was clean and used only by us. And though our bathtub was in the kitchen for some reason, at least we *had* a bathtub—as well as a kitchen. Thanks to rent control and a long line of forgeries, the rent was incredibly low, just a hundred forty-eight dollars a month. For decades, it seemed, a succession of tenants had been faithfully impersonating the woman who'd lived here back in the 1940s, paying the rent each month with money orders signed in her name.

Laura surprised me by throwing herself into keeping house, cooking the fried liver and onions dish she remembered her mother making and sweeping the kitchen floor by using one of her mother's tricks (wetting the edge of a newspaper sheet so that it stuck to the floor and served as a homemade dustpan). Money was very, very tight. Though Uncle Ed paid our rent and I continued to work evenings for the gay stockbroker, Laura and I seemed to be living right at—or was it right below?—the poverty line. When we did eat out it was always at Blimpies, the submarine sandwich shop, because I remembered my uncle stressing the importance of eating at least one green vegetable per day. (I had a harder time putting into practice other food and drink advice from him, such as that sweets are only for children and old men; that upper-class people prefer their meat rare; and that when buying cheap wine one should go with Chablis because cheap Burgundy "tastes like gasoline.")

Now that we'd set up house downtown we hardly saw Uncle Ed anymore. We were lucky to see him once a week for dinner at his apartment. Though I knew I was hardly in a position to complain—how many teenagers got to live with their girlfriend in their own Manhattan apartment?—I still couldn't help regretting how winning Laura had also turned out to mean losing him. Perhaps Uncle Ed had been right when he'd said, with that cheerfulness he always used to make his bleakest pronouncements, that in life "every gain is also usually a loss."

Years later my uncle would tell me that he'd made a conscious decision to remove himself from our daily lives; he felt Laura and I had clashed so often with adults that we were best left to ourselves in a world cleared of all authority figures. But I think he may have been overestimating my problems with authority— at least with authorities like him. He himself, in any event, was so hypersensitive about being perceived as an oppressive adult that I remember how astounded I was when he told me that during the visit my Free School friend Donny and I paid him in Greenwich Village as fourteen-year-olds, he'd been "terrified" of our "scorn." I don't know what I found more astounding: that he'd think we could ever feel scornful of him or that our scorn would matter so much. I also think my uncle always *under*estimated how indebted to him I felt—and how devoted.

Late that summer it came time to choose a prep school. With the Tutoring School having rehabilitated my transcript to the point where I was now only a year behind my age group, Uncle Ed looked around and came up with two schools not quite so forbiddingly expensive as better-known places like Trinity and Horace Mann. The final decision was up to me, he said. When he was a teenager he'd hated it when his father, E.V., had chosen his prep school for him, sending him to the Cranbrook Boys' School outside Detroit simply because it lay on the route between E.V.'s winter and summer homes. As I weighed my two choices—an arty, progressive Quaker school in the East Village, and a much stodgier place, complete with British faculty, on the Upper West Side—I happened to hear my uncle speculating one night that the East Village school was "probably the kind of place where if you show up late for class they just say you're being 'creative.'" This stinging characterization clinched my decision for me on the spot. The East Village place suddenly sounded all too much like the Free School and the last thing I wanted was to become the sort of undisciplined, self-indulgent artist type that Uncle Ed seemed to enjoy mocking above all others.

Secretly, I was also attracted to the stodgy school's dress code. Boys at Franklin School had to wear a "coat and tie" (a phrase I'd never heard before) and the prospect of acquiring what my parents called "dress-up clothes" excited me. My uncle took me to Barney's Basement, the discount men's store, where he immediately selected a blond tweed jacket from the rack, explaining as I put it on that the handiest way of judging whether a jacket was the right size was to let your arm hang down at your side: the jacket should extend exactly to the knuckle of your thumb. He said that classic styles, such as tweed jackets, never go out of fashion and that the jackets here at Barney's were all

European cut—"tapered"—so that instead of looking like the "shapeless potato sacks" worn by so many American men, these jackets were cut so that they slanted in from shoulder to waist in the shape of a V. "By the way, one should never wear a brown suit after dark," my uncle warned me, and I dutifully made a mental note of this even though I owned no suits of any kind, including brown. By the time we walked out of Barney's I had three new jackets and three pairs of trousers that the tailor, his mouth dangerously stuffed with pins, had altered for me after spearing in place the creases he'd marked with his stick of chalk on the comically long trouser legs pooling at my feet.

Back at our apartment Laura had me try on everything for her because she wanted to see how my ass looked in the new pants. I knew she was jealous of my new clothes and new school, and I was glad when Uncle Ed now turned his attention to her. He thought it would be nice if she attended a Catholic school in the city, but the problem was how would he represent himself to the school authorities when he went to enroll her? The solution came to him at a party one night when he happened to meet Claudia, a former Miss Venezuela. Claudia was now about thirty and living in Little Italy with a writer boyfriend whom my uncle knew faintly. He invited the couple to dinner at his apartment and by the end of the meal he'd convinced Claudia to enroll Laura by posing as her aunt.

Because the girls at Laura's new school wore a uniform (white blouse, gray dress) there was no need to buy her any clothes, but one night I came home to find Laura lounging around in the kitchen in a glamorous new outfit. It seemed Uncle Ed had called her up and said, "Let's you and me go shopping—I want to be your fairy godmother." He took her to Charivari, the trendy Italian shop, where he told the saleswoman: "Whatever you think. We have this great party to go to." Laura wound up selecting loose, bell-bottomish slacks, a silk blouse, and open-toed platform shoes with ankle ties. She told me she was touched that "Teddy" had "spent all this money" on her; my uncle for his part said it was fun to be treated by the Charivari saleswoman as though he were Laura's heterosexual sugar daddy. "New Yorkers are so quick to ascribe sexual motives to generosity," he said with a smile.

Because my uncle liked to bestow his generosity impulsively, when the spirit moved him, I suppose it made sense that he'd be bad at honoring anything hollow and official. For when it came to remembering things like Christmas and birthdays, he was hopeless. He'd bought Laura her Charivari outfit because she'd charmed him by telling him about the *quinsiñeta*, the Spanish celebration of a girl's fifteenth birthday when her father throws her a big party. But though he'd fantasized aloud about giving her a *quinsiñeta* and dancing the big dance with her that father and daughter traditionally performed, by the time Laura's fifteenth birthday actually rolled around that fall it had all slipped his mind. The one exception to his forgetfulness about birthdays was his mother's birthday in early October. Though he'd confided to me that he felt like "a sitting duck" whenever she came to town and that "Mother and her big mouth can be so embarrassing," he proceeded to arrange for her to fly into New York the weekend of her birthday. My tiny grandmother, beaming and wearing the navy blue Neiman Marcus dress she'd bought with the birthday check he'd sent her, wasted no time in embarrassing us. Introducing herself to Laura, my grandmother exclaimed, "You're Mexican? Why, honey, we used to have a maid once who was Mexican."

Even more embarrassing was the big Sunday brunch we all attended at a high-rise apartment near the United Nations Secretariat. My uncle said the only reason our host, a rich, balding Texan named Jesse, had invited us was that Jesse regarded us all as "sort of like Keith McDermott's family." Jesse was such a big fan of Keith's that he'd lost track of the number of *Equus* performances he'd attended. With a big repulsive smile he told us that all those front row tickets he'd bought added up to quite a pretty penny but that it was "worth every dime to see him naked" (Keith had a brief nude scene in the play). Jesse had placed cards next to each of our plates on the long linen-covered dining table and my grandmother's card read: "Delilah: the only real girl here"—something she was happy to read aloud to the appreciative table of twelve (everyone else seemed to be gay except for me, Laura, and my grandmother). While everyone was laughing away, I privately wondered how it could have been overlooked that Laura was actually the only real girl here.

My grandmother was getting terribly drunk—as were we all. The afternoon sun poured in through the large windows overlooking the East River, dazzling the Chablis in our glasses, which Jesse kept refilling with an almost fanatical zeal. I'd never seen a host so continually on his feet, pouring and urging everyone on. After a while Laura had to go lie down in the master bedroom. But the wine and being at the center of so much male attention only fired my grandmother to new heights of animation. She'd started flirting more and more ardently with our host and I wondered if she'd forgotten he was gay. When it came time for us to wobble to the door and take our leave, I'll never forget the struggle Uncle Ed went through trying to pry loose his mother from the drunken hug she'd fastened onto Jesse. As my uncle told me later, "Except for the fact he's gay, Jesse's everything Mother's looking for in a man: rich, genial . . . generous with his bar."

Now that he had two kids in private school and two rents to pay, my uncle started casting around for a better way to make a living than ghostwriting that U.S. history textbook. When I stopped by his apartment one day I found him typing up something titled "Ten Ways to a Taut Tummy." *Cosmopolitan* magazine was looking for a new editor, he explained, and applicants were supposed to cook up their own mock issues. "Why not?" he told me with a brave shrug. "Oscar Wilde once edited something called *Woman's World*, you know."

After a series of interviews he was told he was one of two finalists. But when he went in for a final interview with Helen Gurley Brown herself, he was unable to answer to her satisfaction the question: "What do you as a gay man know about man-woman fucking?"

But then, out of the blue, Uncle Ed landed a high-paying job through Jesse, who'd recommended him for an executive position at the multinational chemical corporation where Jesse served as a consultant. My uncle, unfamiliar with corporate life, was dismayed to learn that his workday extended not from nine to five, as he'd anticipated, but from eight to eight. His boss, one of the few token women in the company, seemed threatened by his arrival on the scene. As someone adept at charming those around him, Ed found it a new kind of hell to realize that no matter what he did there would be no pleasing his boss. If he did a mediocre job, she screamed at him. If he did a good job (such as when the chairman of the board raved about Ed's ten-page summary of *The Coming of Post-Industrial Society*), his boss seethed with jealousy because she worried he had his eye on her job. It didn't help my uncle's spirits any that one of the corporation's products for children had been catching on fire recently, or that when he'd tried to bring on board a gay friend of his as a freelance photographer, his boss nixed the idea because, as she put it, "*That* kind of person could never be presented to the brass on the thirty-eighth floor."

While Uncle Ed slaved away at the chemical corporation, getting more and more miserable, Laura and I flew back to Chicago for Christmas with my mother. We all called my uncle up on Christmas Eve and when it was my turn on the phone with him, he told me, "Isn't it funny how your mother's welcoming Laura home now like one of the family when six months ago she was throwing her out?" My grandmother also welcomed Laura with open arms. Laura told me she hadn't been offended by Delilah's remark about once having a Mexican maid because, "You can tell when people are being malicious, and she wasn't. Your grandmother just doesn't know any better." Laura actually found my grandmother to be "so bubbly and cute"—this loquacious little old lady tooling along in her big Cadillac and her mink coat. When we went to Delilah's Michigan "country house" for the weekend, Laura got a kick out of how my grandmother had to stop at "her" Howard Johnson's on the way there for yet another highball. But being accepted by my mother and grand-mother around the Christmas tree made Laura homesick for her own family. Late one afternoon I found a note from her on the kitchen table: "Sorry, I got cold feet. I'll be back later."

When she came back that night her face was all aglow from having seen her mother. She'd called *Mamá* up on impulse be-cause she'd begun to worry that being absorbed into my family meant leaving her own family permanently behind. Since run-ning away to New York Laura had often wondered how her mother felt—had she forgotten about her or did she still care?—and over the past few months she'd written *Mamá* a couple let-ters that she'd handed over to "Aunt" Claudia, who'd posted them from Washington, D.C., while on weekend trips there so that the postmark wouldn't reveal Laura's real location. Now, tonight, her mother answered the phone and sounded all excited to hear from Laura. And though she insisted on meeting Laura in front of the House of the Good Shepherd for some reason, it all went fine—it was dark and Sister Dominic was probably already asleep inside the convent. Laura and her mother drove around for hours in her mother's big old Oldsmobile, having a great talk, and then her mother dropped her off back in front of Good Shepherd. What a strange family she had, I thought. For I wondered just what her mother could have been thinking as she permitted her runaway, fifteen-year-old daughter to re-turn to her mysterious life. Perhaps it had something to do with Laura's scary father not wanting her back. When I asked Laura about her dad, she made a face and said he probably thought she'd become a whore and heroin addict.

It never occurred to me to see or telephone my own father while I was in town. I didn't send him a Christmas card either because my mother told me that the previous Christmas, when I was locked up at the Edge, she'd asked Dad over the phone,

"Aren't you even planning to have the kid home for Christmas?" and he'd replied, "No, we're not."

Alone among the parents in our lives, Uncle Ed shouldered the burden of supporting me and Laura. We saw him less than ever now because shortly after we flew back from Chicago Ed's boss assigned him the monumental task of preparing the annual company report for the April shareholders' meeting. But one night our doorbell rang and it was he. It was a haunting little visit I'll never forget because as my haggard uncle swept into our apartment in his businessman's camel hair coat, he spotted a paperback novel in my hand and snapped, "God, I wish *I* had time to read these days." What a relief when Uncle Ed was suddenly able to quit his horrible job right in the middle of doing that company report. He and his friend Chuck Silverstein had landed a contract to write *The Joy of Gay Sex* together and my uncle's share of the advance would be large enough to support us all for the time being.

But even with Uncle Ed now happily back home at his desk I was lucky to see him one or two hours a week for dinner, always with Laura in tow. For me the great irony was that I never saw my uncle alone anymore, even though my prep school was just three short blocks away from his apartment building. Sometimes after school I'd walk down Columbus Avenue and stare up at the windows of his apartment. My life had become surprisingly bleak and lonely. The night Laura and I came back from Christmas in Chicago I'd been shocked by how melancholy Eighth Avenue looked in the slow-falling snow as we made our way past the cheap colored lights strung up on the bodegas and shoe-repair shops, carrying bundles of dirty clothes to the Laundromat. Though Uncle Ed had joked that no one would want to hear that life was anything but paradise for two teens with a Manhattan love nest of their own, Laura and I felt so isolated much of the time in our studio apartment that it was more like living in a little cabin in the woods.

Neither of us had made any real friends our own age. My

prep-school classmates were hard to get to know, hailing taxis or disappearing down subway stairs the minute school let out. Of course, I felt separated from my classmates anyway, unable to tell them I'd come to New York from a bughouse or that I'd gone from living with a gay uncle to keeping house with a fifteen-year-old girl. Many a morning I rushed into nine o'clock English class a few minutes late, my dick still damp from giving Laura the morning screw she sometimes tempted me into, full of the feeling that I lived in a world very much apart from other kids. Still, it was these vagaries of our lives that bound me and Laura together. We were fellow freaks who lived outside the norm and even the law (theoretically, I was a runaway myself, since my custody still officially belonged to my father). In our cramped and unending togetherness Laura and I couldn't help but grow bored with each other, sometimes bickering and even fighting nastily. There were good times too, and always great sex, but in the evenings our tiny apartment could seem divided into two worlds, with me in the glare of the kitchen doing my homework on a board atop the bathtub, and Laura in the flickering dark of the bedroom, giggling at *Mary Hartman, Mary Hartman* on our little TV.

I can't remember exactly when I first noticed it. I know it surprised me how enthusiastic my uncle got when I asked him for help with preparing for the Scholastic Aptitude Test. Suddenly he began inviting me over for lunch all the time, going over with me not only the English part of the test, as I'd expected, but the math part too. As he tutored me, he became increasingly sour on my prep school's preparation of me, until finally he declared my school was just like the one he'd attended—"You know: this pseudointellectual, very British sort of place. There's all this pretending to be interested in knowledge, in intellectual life, but in fact they don't want you to study too much. Their ideal student is actually someone who's mad for sports and has to be scolded to crack the books once in a while."

These lunchtime sessions with Uncle Ed were a lot like the old days with him before Laura came on the scene, with the difference that I began to sense something new, something extra, to his attentions. Hard as it was to believe, my uncle seemed to have a little crush on me. The thought of it made me feel self-conscious, uneasy, and important all at once. Perhaps it was just my imagination—I mean, why would he have a crush on me? But when I showed up in some new chino pants one day, there was new bite to the embarrassment I felt when he asked me to stand up and turn around before his appraising eye (the verdict: I was too skinny). Or when he told me my chin was better than his (stronger, not dimpled), as were my lips (fuller). But most embarrassing of all was the time I was heading back to school up Columbus Avenue and couldn't shake the oppressive feeling of my uncle's eyes still being on me. Sure enough, when I turned around there he was, staring down at me from his sixth-floor study window.

One day out of the blue he asked if I'd like to fly down to Puerto Rico with him during my spring break. "I think we can just swing it," he said, explaining that because he was still waiting for his *Joy of Gay Sex* advance money to arrive in the mail, his checking account was down to five hundred dollars. My feelings about going off with my uncle must have been completely engulfing because for the life of me I can't remember what on earth we told Laura, or what her reaction was. She must have been furiously jealous, and very hurt, about being left behind.

With funds so low, Uncle Ed had gotten hold of plane tickets through a friend that weren't quite kosher. "Not to worry, though," he assured me, "we'll just make sure we're very casual as we go through boarding." We arrived without a hitch in San Juan late in the afternoon, and as we strolled through the open-air terminal he pointed out the absence of walls. "In the tropics there's this breaking down of the distinction between outdoors and indoors," he explained. By sunset, which he pointed out occurred with "sinful speed" at this latitude, the red sun not so much sinking as plopping down all at once below the ocean horizon, we were sauntering barefoot on the *playa publica*, the public beach, each sipping from a plastic cup of rum punch.

After dinner my uncle guided us into a four-star hotel, through the hushed lobby with its overhanging chandeliers, and out the other side. He said that all his life he'd taken pride in trespassing through expensive places and being taken for someone who belonged there. At a palm tree in front of our modest guest house he told me gently, "Okay, kiddo, I'm going to go cruising now. Here's twenty dollars to do whatever you're going to do."

My uncle's example made it seem unadventurous and cowardly for me just to go back to our room and read, so I forced myself to head out in search of some nightlife. He'd told me that in nearby Old San Juan it wasn't nearly so touristy and over there I found a small disco filled with local señoritas. At the bar I ordered a piña colada, then another, and after an hour of agonizing finally approached the girl I'd decided was least likely to refuse me, a girl who looked older and more sisterly than the other girls.

"*Te quieres bailar conmigo?*"—Do you want to dance with me?—I asked her, using the familiar tense because I remembered Laura had said that young Latinos no longer bothered with the formal *you*.

"Maybe later," she said in English.

I was still awake reading in my twin bed when my uncle came in exclaiming, "Guess who I ran into? Your friend Rick!" Rick was someone whose life kept intersecting mine in the funniest way. At eighteen, he was doing the eleventh grade for the third time and by pure coincidence he'd happened to follow me from the Tutoring School to Franklin School. Handsome in a careless, rumpled sort of way, with teeth already deeply stained from cigarettes, Rick had the kind of easygoing worldliness that I was starting to give up hope of ever acquiring. It didn't surprise me to hear that he was down here on his own. "I'm winding through the streets of Old San Juan," my uncle was saying, "you know, paved with those beautiful old blue bricks, and I'm looking for another, for a better, gay bar, and suddenly I hear, 'Mr. White! Mr. White!' I turn around and there's Rick walking up to me with that lopsided grin of his. He's really very sweet, though, Rick. He asked me to have a drink with him but I lied and said I had to get back to you. He says hi."

Soon Uncle Ed was gently snoring in his bed. I'd never slept in the same room with him before and it surprised me how he'd fallen asleep right away even though I still had the light on, reading. It surprised me because over the past year he'd often told me, whenever I'd complain about my insomnia, that he had trouble sleeping too. Perhaps he'd taken some powerful sleeping pill while in the bathroom.

In the morning I told my uncle I'd meet him out on the beach, less because I felt too sleepy to get up than because I didn't want to climb out of bed in front of him in my underwear. I found him on a towel in the hot, dirty-looking sand of the *playa publica*. For my sake he was staying here among the families on the public beach instead of seeking out a gay beach. As we "basted," as he put it, in the sun, he told me that if I lived down here all the time my acne would disappear completely. Then he drew my attention to some sullen native men avoiding the sun by sitting in the shade of bushes back away from the beach. He said they no doubt loathed us tourists, even if they might desire some of us. Always a fountain of startling information, my uncle, now that I had him to myself (and never had I had him so much to myself, not a phone in sight), kept the information flowing and flowing into my brain. Did I know that *Romeo and Juliet's* famous line "Wherefore art thou, Romeo?" actually means not *where* are you, Romeo, but *why* are you Romeo—why do you, Romeo, have to be from the very clan my family is feuding with? Or that when pre-twentieth-century authors use the phrase *making love*, they're talking about flirting, not fucking? (This had in fact puzzled me in my reading; I'd wondered, for instance, how the young nobleman could have dared to make love to the girl in front of so many other people at the ball, including her own parents.) Or did I know that impotence can be considered a form of performance anxiety, in the same league as stage fright? The most effective therapy, consequently, is one that takes all the pressure off the would-be performer by pretending there will be no performance. In other words, the two partners agree beforehand that they're just going to fool around this time, they're not going to have sex, with the result of course that they do have sex. "You see, neurologically, impotence is caused by a kind of short-circuiting," my uncle concluded. "The sympathetic nervous system (erections) can't operate if the *para*sympathetic nervous system (anxiety) is operating."

When we'd had enough of the beach my uncle and I went back to our room to shower and change (I changed in the bathroom). After lunch, we went off to try and find my classmate Rick but soon gave up. My uncle said he must have gotten the place Rick was staying wrong. We were now crossing a tiled plaza, sunbaked and dirty and busy with pigeons. My uncle noticed that a whitewashed church was for sale and said, "Wouldn't it be great to live in your own little church?" A moment later I made one of my all-time idiotic remarks. We were discussing God—or rather, the absence of God—when I said, "But if there's no God then how did we get here?" In the pause that followed my uncle must have been wondering how on earth I could have gone to school all these years without ever hearing about Darwin's theory of evolution, which he proceeded to fill me in on. I knew it wore Uncle Ed out when I brought a serious, burrowing mood to our talks. I knew he preferred conversation to be mostly lighthearted, open to the air, but now that I had his ear for long stretches of time I couldn't resist falling into that earnestness about issues that I'd once heard him characterize as "high-schooly." Of course, I *was* a high school student, and if my uncle didn't have "all the answers"—as he'd told me, exasperated, that one time—he did have quite a few of them.

Uncle Ed seemed to have made it a point to turn the whole day over to me, and yet his crush (if there'd ever really been one) had disappeared down here in Puerto Rico as mysteriously as it came. I kept picking up a sense of interior distance in him, a sense that he was going through the motions with me, marking time, doing his duty. The signs of restlessness I knew so well in him—the eyes flicking elsewhere as I talked, the thumb and fingers of his right hand rubbing together in the "money" gesture—reminded me that the meter was running. For the remainder of our trip he kept us very busy. There was the ragged little parade we came upon, something to do with the sea, little children marching along dressed up as sea horses. And at dusk there was the public square we walked into where old men sat around in their undershirts watching a large TV placed in the crook of a tree. For dinner we changed into coats and ties and my uncle told me that putting on formal clothing after a day on the beach, slipping into a snowy-white starched shirt with your skin still smarting from exposure to the sun, was one of his favorite things in life. He liked how one's newly tanned hands seemed to glow against the brilliant shirt cuffs.

Now that he'd pointed out the effect, I kept staring at my glowing brown hands that evening as I played blackjack. Uncle Ed had parked me at a fancy hotel casino, giving me fifty dollars for chips and telling me he'd be back in a couple hours, that it would probably take about that long for me to lose everything. He was right on the money. When he returned we headed down to the waterfront, where we had a rum punch at a raunchy sailor's bar. At one point a frizzy-haired young prostitute climbed up onto my lap and propositioned me by saying, "Fucky-fucky, sucky-sucky?" Somehow she knew not to climb onto my uncle's lap.

Back out in the soft tropical night we passed a flock of heavily rouged prostitutes standing around outside a big hotel (these ones did proposition Ed). We stopped for another drink, a nightcap, my uncle called it, at a very quiet little bar. The subject of his mother, my grandmother, came up. It had always mystified me how much he doted on her, faithfully telephoning her once a week in Chicago, and in my seventeen-year-old innocence I came right out and told him I thought there was something "a little funny" about his relationship with her. "Oh, really," he said. Yes, I went on, there was something in his regard for her that didn't add up, that seemed all out of proportion to who she was. I was laughing good-naturedly, thinking it shouldn't be too hard to get him to see the light. I was even enjoying how, for once, *I* had something to point out to *him*. I had such faith in his sharpness about everything that it never occurred to me this one blind spot I thought I'd detected in him would remain stubbornly blind. I kept expecting him to say, with his wonderful candor, his way of grasping things instantly, that, yes, come to think of it I was right, what could he have been thinking?

Instead, I saw him stiffen and in the silence that grew around him I let the subject drop.

On our way back to the guest house he pointed out a circular stone bench that looked invitingly shadowy under dreamy, overhanging trees: "When I was your age I was always wanting to sit in places like that and talk all night about life and love and what it all means," he said. "Now of course I couldn't be less interested."

I'd heard him say similar things before. When a dinner guest at the apartment made the mistake of staying on too deep into the evening and unburdening himself too extensively, the guest was sure to be criticized as "juvenile" afterward by my uncle and Keith McDermott as they washed and dried the dinner plates. Ed and Keith would agree that they no longer had any patience for heart-to-heart talks, which were pointless as well as exhausting. They'd declare, in the spirit of Oscar Wilde, that everything of interest could be found right on the surface of things and that to start probing something almost guaranteed a tedious conversation. And yet for all this I'd noticed that in daily life my uncle was too flexible to stick to all his opinions. He did still have heart-to-heart talks sometimes, apparently, for I remember that not long after we flew back to New York from San Juan he recounted for me how he'd picked up a guy on Christopher Street, gone home with him to have sex, and then "talked until dawn" with him on the guy's futon. "The usual courtship rituals are being completely reversed," he told me, looking delighted. "Instead of getting to know someone before you go to bed with them, the new thing is to have sex before knowing each other's names and only afterward tell each other the story of your lives."

Pestering him with questions one day, I learned that my uncle's most fundamental position of all was that it's human nature to be full of contradictions. Coexisting inside us all, he said, are beliefs that are totally at odds with, if often unaware of, one another. "Take you and me, for instance," he said. "On a philosophical level we say that life is meaningless and yet at the same time we also think it's really important to get an A in class or a good review in the *Times*."

It was only in light of human contradiction, of my uncle's contradictions, that I could even begin to understand his surprising choice of new boyfriend. For that spring of 1977 Uncle Ed took up with a guy named Rudy—the first regular boyfriend he'd had since I'd come to New York. I knew how much looks mattered to my uncle and it struck me as weird to see him now with Rudy, a big, friendly man with a grizzled beard and hair so close-cropped it was like a five o'clock shadow on his skull. But the only thing my uncle ever said to me about Rudy's lack of looks was that seeing such a man represented a big step forward for him "because only confident people dare to be seen with someone less than beautiful." I couldn't help wondering, though, if this wasn't just putting a brave face on things, and if Rudy wasn't just a shabby substitute for Keith McDermott, whose presence around the apartment continued to haunt Ed.

For one thing, it sometimes seemed that Laura and I saw more of Rudy than my uncle did. Rudy worked at the Pleasure Chest, a gay sex shop hard by the Hudson River at the far end of Christopher Street. When Rudy met us he'd told me and Laura to feel free to come on by the shop anytime and hang out with him there, and in our boredom and loneliness Laura and I started taking him up on this. What we liked about Rudy was how, unlike Uncle Ed, he was always available. With his glasses and gummy, goofy grin, Rudy was as calm, sweet-tempered, and unambitious as a housewife at a bake sale. He manned the Pleasure Chest from four to midnight and on weekend nights we'd while away the hours chatting with him—Rudy standing there at the cash register in his "butch" costume of black boots and jeans outfitted with key rings dangling from several belt loops, Laura and I lighting up cigarettes and leaning against the glass cases displaying cock rings, whips, dildos, and leather harnesses. The sex shop's front room was never very busy because almost every "customer" who walked in immediately drifted toward and then through the curtained doorway at the back. They had entered, Rudy told us, the small, completely dark "orgy room" back there.

But somehow none of the hard-core paraphernalia and goings-on at the Pleasure Chest ever bothered me at all, I guess because none of it seemed quite real. Just as when I was twelve and found out Uncle Ed was gay, I was able to avoid dwelling on the graphic reality. I never imagined anyone actually using the sex toys on display and the orgy supposedly going on in the back room might as well have been a bunch of neighbors playing poker. It all carried so little weight in both Laura's and my mind that we were only happy to wear the blue tank tops Rudy gave us emblazoned with the name of a gay bar, the Toilet, above a drawing of a big toilet. We just thought they were cool. We wore them as something that amused us, not as anything reflecting the physical reality of what went on at a notorious downtown fist-fucking bar.

No doubt a big part of being able to feel so blasé about the Pleasure Chest was having Laura there at my side. But late that spring she made a shocking decision that threw everything up in the air. I guess I'd been taking her for granted for quite a while now—or rather, we'd both been getting a bit sick of each other, as though a year of domestic life had aged our relationship into something closer to a twenty-year marriage. But part of my boredom was my certainty that she and I would go on living together for as far as I could see into the future. Where else would we go? And who else could we expect to understand us? We were "trench mates," as my uncle put it, who'd survived Dr. Schwarz and now shared the same funny status as wards of Uncle Ed adrift between the worlds of kids and adults, gays and straights.

Yet Laura had been feeling even lonelier than I'd been aware of. Sometimes she'd show up at the Merrill Lynch office to help me with my endless envelope stuffing so that I could get out of there early enough for us to see a movie together. But most evenings she'd be home alone staring at the exposed brick walls of our living room/bedroom. She'd discovered that the very good-looking man across the hall from us made his living as a hustler. Several times a night she'd hear him buzzing someone in through the front door, and when she looked out our door's peephole there would be our neighbor standing bare-chested in his open doorway, wearing only boxer shorts. An hour later she'd hear him saying good-bye to his male visitor/customer.

But what frustrated Laura more than anything was that just as she'd been getting to be pretty good friends with "Aunt" Claudia, Claudia abruptly decided to leave New York and get married to some rich guy down in Venezuela. When my uncle and I had gone off to Puerto Rico, Laura had hung out at Claudia's apartment in Little Italy, drinking wine spritzers and eating the chunks of mozzarella cheese on which Claudia liked to sprinkle ground pepper. And it was Claudia who gave Laura some jackets and skirts she'd set aside while cleaning out her closets. Claudia had also been the one who advised Laura to start using the brown lipstick that had just become fashionable and that went so well with their dark coloring.

"So when Claudia said she was leaving it was kind of the last straw," Laura explained. For her big news was that when she'd met her mother in front of the convent over Christmas, they'd actually driven down to the south side of Chicago where her mother showed her the house into which the family, after years of cramped living in the little apartment in Wicker Park, would be moving in six months. Laura's mother promised her a great new life in the new house, and Laura was inspired to think that maybe she really could begin anew with her family, and on a much better footing this time. For they finally seemed to appreciate her now that she'd run away from them. At least her mother did. And yet in Laura's strange family any definite decision about Laura's rejoining the family was put off till later. And Laura hadn't wanted to mention any of this to me till she'd made up her mind for sure.

It didn't take long for me to decide I wanted to go back to Chicago too. I called up my mother and was secretly glad to hear that Mom and Phyllis, after three years of living together, had decided to call it quits. Glad, because my mother told me she'd been dreading the idea of living by herself and would love for me to come live with her. I could even attend Evanston High for my senior year, she said, growing more excited. Because though I'd be residing with her in Chicago in the new little apartment on Foster Avenue she was moving into, why should I have to go to some run-down, dangerous Chicago public high school? No, what we would do is register me at Evanston High by claiming I'd moved back in with my father and stepmother. Then I'd just commute to school each day on the El.

I can't remember now the scene where Laura and I told Uncle Ed that we'd both decided to go back to Chicago to our mothers. I think we must have told him during the weekend we went to Fire Island late that May. Rudy came along too and on the ferry ride across the bay I remember Rudy telling Ed how he thought Laura and I were living on too little money. Then my uncle told us all how sick he was of being too busy *writing* about the joy of gay sex to experience any joy himself. For the past several weeks he and his chubby, bearded cowriter, Chuck Silverstein, had been holed up in their separate apartments trying to finish *The Joy of Gay Sex*; now it was nearly done. Uncle Ed said he'd decided to sign his real name to it, which meant that when his father, whose full name was also Edmund White, got wind of the thing it was probably going to send his already high blood pressure through the roof. (When *The Joy of Gay Sex* did come out later that year, there were rumors in the family—totally unfounded rumors, as it turned out—that E.V. was so shocked to read about his son's shameful book in his Sunday Cincinnati *Enquirer* that it precipitated his final, fatal heart attack a short time later. Knowing that E.V.'s first heart attack had been brought on by his bike race with me, my uncle couldn't resist telling me while in a playful mood one night, "I guess you softened him up and then I finished him off.")

That weekend was Laura's and my only visit to Fire Island and we were charmed by the little red wagon provided by the dockside grocery store to roll our bags of expensive groceries to the house where we were staying, more than a mile away. As we made our way single file along the narrow wooden walkway raised up on stilts above the dunes, my uncle stopped at one point to point out some nondescript scrub brush and pines down below. This, he said, was the famous "meat rack." Here, after dark, an outdoor orgy took place every weekend night. Apparently more than one participant had passed out on drugs in the cold meat-rack sand only to be awakened in the dawn by wild deer licking the semen off his naked flesh.

It's funny how stray details about that Fire Island weekend come easily to mind but nothing about my uncle's reaction to our leaving town. I can remember the silhouettes of people walking the lonely, winding walkways at night, their orange cigarette tips glowing; or my uncle saying "this poor stoned boy" when I asked him in front of some poolside friends the next day whether aliens would be able to recognize the dominant animal on earth if just shown some pictures of monkeys, people, and big cats.

Perhaps Uncle Ed didn't have much of a reaction when we told him. I know that I couldn't have said much more to him than, "Well, since Laura's going back, I guess I am too," because in years to come my uncle would always attribute my departure to "not being able to live without Laura." In fact there were other reasons that, out of embarrassment, shyness, and even a sense of protectiveness toward him, I never mentioned. Manhattan, for instance, already seemed bleak enough with Laura at my side; to stay on without her, even if that meant moving back into my old maid's room, struck me as an unbearably lonely prospect. Then too, Laura had never spoken about wanting to leave *me*—only New York. Domestic life had killed our romance but who was to say that living apart and just dating each other again wouldn't rekindle things between us?

I also yearned to be back with my Evanston friends. For more than a year now I'd been waiting to feel I'd outgrown them and at last put my "provincial" past behind me. But in the weeks leading up to Christmas vacation it had surprised me how obsessively I was looking forward to going to Chicago; I wouldn't have wanted to admit it, but it had become what I was living for. Now enough time had gone by for me to realize that, as much as I'd changed under Uncle Ed, these old friends of mine were still my only real friends—the one constant throughout the upheavals of the past few years. I missed my friends so much, in fact, that it ended up costing me my job. I'd gotten in the habit of staying late at the Merrill Lynch office so that I could call them up in Evanston on the office WATS (long distance) line after all the stockbrokers had gone home. But just before the Fire Island weekend I'd finally gotten caught. A stockbroker returned unexpectedly to the office at ten P.M. and found me sitting in his cubicle in the back, talking long distance with my feet up on his desk. My gay stockbroker employer, already jumpy about his own status in such a conservative office, felt he couldn't risk any friction on my account and had to let me go. Though he lived with his lover in the Village and rented a summer place in the gay Fire Island Pines, he'd constructed a whole fictional identity for himself at work, complete with Long Island wife and home. I'd often heard him saying loudly into his phone, for the benefit of eavesdropping colleagues, "Honey, I'm running late. I'm going to try to catch the six oh five." My uncle said it was ridiculous that "the Goon"—Uncle Ed's cruel nickname for my employer—went to such elaborate lengths to cover himself, since "the Goon is big, balding, and bearded—all things that count as 'straight' among straight people."

My uncle didn't like good-byes, didn't like making a production out of them. And so on the sunny June morning of Laura's and my departure he came by our apartment only at the last minute. Laura and I had been hauling stuff out to the street and our male-prostitute neighbor across the hall, hearing all the commotion, poked his head out the door. Uncle Ed started chatting with him (did they know each other?) and before long we were all carrying Laura's and my double bed into this guy's apartment. His old bed was all worn out, I guess. Then, with what seemed to me excessive, even irritating urgency, my uncle was hustling Laura and me out the door, telling us, "C'mon, you two—you're going to miss your plane." He probably was genuinely worried we'd get snarled in traffic on the way to the airport but it was hard not to feel, as he ran out into the middle of Fifteenth Street to make sure the taxi stopped for us, that he couldn't get rid of us a moment too soon.

I'm just like my uncle in the way I go kind of numb and move mechanically through the "big" moments of life. I guess he must have given us each a quick hug and Laura and I must have thanked him for everything . . . all I remember is turning around in the backseat as the taxi lurched forward and seeing that my uncle, who didn't believe in standing around and waving, was already heading down the sidewalk away from us.

CHAPTER 7

BACK IN THE PROVINCES

I hadn't seen my father in nearly two years—not since the November night he'd delivered me back to Dr. Schwarz at Riveredge Hospital. But the night before my reunion with Dad, I dreamt he was driving me somewhere in an old Volkswagen Beetle. This car had so little horsepower that we could barely putter up the ramp to the highway. And when we did get up there, we found ourselves driving into the teeth of oncoming traffic— we'd gone up the exit ramp by mistake! I'd heard my uncle say that his own dreams could be so simple and transparent sometimes that they were no more than literal illustrations of some old saying. He'd once dreamt, for instance, that he was sailing a dinghy on a lake when a much bigger boat came surging up alongside him, bringing his little dinghy to a standstill. At the helm of the big boat was his father, E.V. The saying? "Taking the wind out of my sails," my uncle said with a wry smile. The meaning of my own Daddy Dream seemed pretty transparent too. While not an illustrated saying, my dream could not have spelled out any more clearly what I thought of my father's whole treatment of me. Dad had tried to take me the wrong way (driving up the exit ramp), although the truth was that he was quite powerless (his strangely hobbled Volkswagen).

This view of my father had crystallized the night I came back to Chicago when my mother and I sat up late, talking. She had some very weird news: my father and stepmother had recently threatened to send my sixteen-year-old sister to a foster home simply because they were hurt by the way she was "ignoring" them lately, spending most of her time at home in her room studying or on the phone. If it hadn't been completely clear before what their game was, Mom said, cackling with glee, it sure was now. For what better proof could there be of my stepmother's dark designs, of her total domination of my father, than this crazy threat to get rid of my mild-mannered sister? "You can bet she was behind all the stuff with you too," my mother went on, referring to my stepmother. "When your doctors wanted to send you home or did send you home, you better believe she was screaming bloody murder to your dad about it. She wanted you out of that house, Keithie, and she wanted it done on the cheap, too. Remember that nice boarding school in Lake Bluff that Dr. Johnson wanted to send you to? Well, let me tell you, it's a whole lot cheaper to keep a kid in the hospital if you've got insurance to cover everything like your dad does."

As to why my stepmother had ever agreed to let us kids come live with them in the first place, my mother believed that some of it had to be naïveté—"I'm sure she had no idea just what she was in for with you all—I mean, what was she back then, twenty-five or -six?" But Stepmom was determined to "one-up" Mom, my mother felt sure, by proving she could be a better wife to

Dad and a better mother to us. "Remember how *keen* they were to get you to agree to live with them, Keithie, promising you the moon?"

When my father reached me on the phone at Mom's a few days later, I told him I was willing to see him but not my stepmother. He decided he and I should meet up at Evanston High, the place he'd had so much trouble getting me to attend in the old days but where I'd now enrolled in summer school classes. He pulled up in his new family van, looking very summery in his tennis whites and with his familiar sunburned nose and bald spot. The first words out of his mouth were, "Hey, you look great. You haven't looked this good since you were twelve." A few minutes later he added how great it was to see me "functioning" again. But the funny thing is that my father never said a word about Uncle Ed, never acknowledged all he'd accomplished with my skin, my school, my attitude. To do so, I guess, would be tantamount to admitting his own handling of me had been wrongheaded (after all, if Mom and Uncle Ed hadn't interceded, I would only now be getting out of the long-term treatment place Dad had been so dead set on sending me to). It was almost as though my father wanted to pretend I was a wild boy who'd gone running off into the forest all covered with sores and had now re-emerged magically healed.

We went to a coffee shop in downtown Evanston and it was very weird to sit there with him acting as though the past two years hadn't happened. He didn't ask a single question about Laura, or my prep school, or our apartment. But then my father had always conducted conversations as though there were land mines everywhere to be avoided. The idea was to work hard at keeping things as normal and tepid as possible. As he plodded on in his droning voice about Grandma Fleming's new job in a bank, the hot weather we were having, and the Chicago Cubs baseball team, it struck me that my father's way of speaking, if not exactly robotic/retarded as my mother had always portrayed it, did come across as though he himself were weary of what he

was saying. It really was hard to believe that this man with the
simple, flat-looking blue eyes was my *father*.

What I would have wanted to ask him if I dared, and I didn't
dare, was how he could have thought that Dr. Schwarz would
ever get me "functioning" again. Because even if you looked
upon me as a malfunctioning machine, as Dad had, would you
try to fix a fucked-up toaster or TV by subjecting it to stress
and shocks and then throwing the thing in cold storage for
months?

Had my father engaged me in a real conversation I also probably would have confessed to him that my functioning these days
was still not glitch free. The past year at prep school, for instance, I'd cut a whole lot of classes. I'd found out I could call
in sick for myself and immediately began abusing the privilege,
missing one and sometimes two days of school a week. It was
the only way I could get a decent night's rest. For I'd discovered
I didn't respond well to pressure, even the "pressure" of having
to go to school each morning. I'd be lying there at three in the
morning and the only thing that could get me to relax was deciding to grant myself permission to sleep in the next day. As
soon as I'd done this, I'd fall asleep instantly. But all my absences
didn't keep me from finishing near the top of my class and the
funny thing was that the other two top students cut as much
school as I did. One was a sort of aspiring Barry Manilow who
wrote and performed songs on a grand piano in his parents'
Upper East Side apartment and the other was his adoring girlfriend. The two of them brought such a cheerful, unassailable
air to playing hooky that it made it more acceptable for all of
us. None of our brisk British teachers ever complained about
our frequent absences.

When I saw my sister she told me I had this glow about me,
this "New York air." And I did find it energizing to have left
the big, intimidating stage of Manhattan behind; I liked the idea
of playing the New Yorker out here in the provinces where there
were no real New Yorkers. One day I put on some of my

Barney's Basement clothes and paraded up and down Michigan Avenue, wondering why the men passing by in their "shapeless potato sacks," as my uncle had called them, didn't just come right up and ask me, "But where did you get that European-cut jacket?"

I didn't wear anything too fancy to my summer-school classes at Evanston High—just a Pierre Cardin shirt, crisply ironed, with the sleeves rolled up the way Uncle Ed did them: two wide folds halfway up the forearms. My uncle had given me a leather duffel bag, a relic from his chemical corporation days that had the company crest tooled into it, and the bag came in handy now that I was riding such long distances on the El every day. I stocked it with books, including Chesterfield's *Letters to His Son*, which I was re-reading. But one morning in the Evanston High hallways two girl classmates came up to me, snickering and pointing at the duffel bag: "What is that, your suitcase?"

Ordinarily, I would have felt wounded for days but now I was feeling too good, riding too high. I loved being back in Evanston, loved going back to my old neighborhood where my friends and I would get high in an upstairs bedroom while listening to the Beatles' *Abbey Road*. The previous summer in Manhattan had been so claustrophobic and depressing—walking the garbage-smelling streets with Laura, waiting hopelessly on the hot, airless subway platforms where there would be no sign of an incoming train's headlights, no matter how deeply we peered into the bowels of the dusty old tunnels—and it was heaven now to be back in green summertime, throwing a Frisbee around under the old elms. The beauty of the El struck me for the first time, really, particularly the long run alongside Graceland Cemetery. From my padded brown vinyl El seat I'd watch as we passed one giant cottonwood tree after another, their tall, twinkling crowns the pale green color of grapes in the sun. Below the line of cottonwoods ran the high stone cemetery wall and I always kept a lookout for the spot on the wall where someone had scrawled A HARD MAN IS GOOD TO FIND in huge letters. For it was right after HARD MAN that the El made a screeching turn to the east as the tracks veered sharply away from the cemetery and the El eased itself into Sheridan Station and its long wooden wharf of a platform. Sheridan Station would always be haunted for me now, bound up in my mind with my mother's old apartment and Laura's convent.

A couple times a week I'd make a long trek down to Laura's family's new house. It was on the southwest side of the city and to get there I had to get off the El in the thick of the South Side ghetto and catch a bus. As the only white person on the Fifty-fifth Street bus, I'd sit all the way in the rear and hide behind a newspaper as the bus crept westward in fits and starts. One blinding summer day I showed up in sunglasses and got a lecture from Laura's sister's boyfriend, a tough-looking Latino guy. He told me never to wear sunglasses on the bus again because black people "don't like it when they can't tell where you be lookin' at. They get all paranoid and shit. They think maybe you be lookin' at them and laughin' to yourself." I took him to speak from personal experience since he himself was wearing sunglasses, and apparently always wore them, the impenetrable, black, wraparound kind that blind people like Ray Charles and José Feliciano wore. In fact, his nickname was "Shades."

I'd been worried about finally meeting Laura's family because I didn't know how she'd explained my relationship with her to them, but they all seemed to accept me. Her sister was just as beautiful but taller and more imperious. Her mother was also tall and thin, a handsome woman with black, dolorous wet eyes and hair swept up in a dignified bun. Because her English was minimal, I never had to answer any pointed questions about my role in her daughter's past. And I was glad Laura's father never seemed to be around when I was there because Laura told me she'd just discovered where he kept his gun, down in the basement. The basement was also where Laura's older brother lived. He was very handsome and suave, though Laura said he spent all his time lounging around in his basement bedroom in a silk dressing gown, watching James Bond movies and imagining he was James Bond. Clumsiness seemed to offend him. For when

I stumbled once on the stairs, he turned around with a vile little smile and said, "What are you—Woody Allen?"

In that house you had to shout to be heard in the living and dining rooms. The stereo and the TV would both be blasting away at each other and Laura's mother kept these rooms so dark, the thick drapes pulled shut against the summer sun, that when I first entered the house I'd always be blind and disoriented. Laura and I would sit down on the sofa, which was protected by plastic sheets, but we couldn't touch each other too intimately because you never knew when a family member might suddenly emerge from the shadows, shouting something at Laura in Spanish. The family had just acquired two large black dogs, Dobermans or rottweilers, I think, and these very active creatures were constantly circulating at a fast trot. Nosing their way out the back screen door, they'd run alongside the house, barking, and then reappear via the front door. They were brothers, I think.

Laura's and my passion seemed to burn brightest in illicit-seeming settings but I never dreamed we'd fuck in such a risky way. True, there was no other way of doing it at her house but I never would have dared to go through with it if she hadn't insisted. After tethering the dogs to the front gate, Laura would throw her arms around me as we stood together in a little brick archway outside the side door to the basement, an archway whose floor was sunk down three steps from the sidewalk. With the dogs barking away, she'd step out of her cutoff jeans. She wore no underwear and we'd start going at it right away, with me lifting and then pressing her up against the door as I thrust myself into her and tried to come as quickly as I could, before we got caught, before my trembling arms gave out from holding up her weight. It would be broad daylight and any one of her family could have come upon us at any time. Somehow we always got away with it, nine or ten times in all. How strange that this risky, exciting sex would be the last we'd ever have.

That summer I began to feel on the brink of a whole new, expansive life. I'd got to know a girl called Kristin while sitting out on the sun-dappled grass in between summer-school classes at Evanston High. Kristin had a serious, honey-blonde Swedish prettiness set in a whole different key from Laura's beauty—elegantly thin arms and legs, cheekbones that stood out with sculptural sharpness on her long face. As we sat there cross-legged, Kristin in a lemon-yellow sundress, I'd catch glimpses of her wholesome white panties. She made me feel wry, seasoned, mysterious, attractive. She'd never lived anywhere but north Evanston and, without being curious about any of the details, she seemed very approving of my having done something as exotic as live in New York City. Still, I never would have thought I could ask her for a date until she told me one day that it would be fun to get together some time outside school.

My uncle had told me it's natural when you've undergone big personal changes to want to jettison the people you knew before—the living witnesses, that is, to your earlier, sorrier state—and to want to replace them with people who know only this newest and best version of yourself. But I'd never wanted to jettison Laura. No, what I proposed to her on the phone one night was the kind of ultramodern arrangement I could imagine Uncle Ed endorsing: she and I would be free to see other people but we'd also continue to see each other. Our relationship, in fact, would remain the primary one; these other people we'd be seeing would just be supplements. We'd follow a don't ask, don't tell policy about them, of course.

But Laura got mad and, before hanging up on me, said that if I wasn't interested in her anymore, then, fine, we'd break up. The next day I asked Kristin if she wanted to get together that evening. She said sure. Then she asked me if I had a car. When I said no, she said she couldn't go out with me unless I had one. My mother, when I asked her that night, told me there was no way I could borrow her car and that she wasn't going to buy me a used one either. In fact, she needed me to go out and get a job to help her make ends meet. She'd decided the time was ripe for her to go into private practice as a therapist, but it would take time to build up a clientele and money would be very tight for a while.

I think my getting a job must have been the last straw for

Laura. Because though we made up a few days after our phone spat, with me assuring her I didn't need to see anyone but her, once I started working that fall I hardly saw her anymore. I'd found a job through Evanston High's work-study program as an assistant to four women selling educational films over the phone. The job was in Wilmette, the next suburb north, and my new daily round now saw me taking the El to school each morning, then the bus to work each afternoon. By the weekend I had no stomach for the ninety-minute train and bus ride to Laura's house. I'd ask her to come down and see me but Laura would say she was too busy with homework. That sounded a little hard to believe but there was never any clear, dramatic moment when I suddenly felt: Oh no, she's slipping away from me for good.

It all just happened so fast.

One night I happened to call up Uncle Ed and Keith Mc-Dermott answered the phone. "We just heard the news," he told me. "God, I'm so sorry. You must feel terrible. Here, let me put your uncle on." My uncle came on the line and I asked him what was up. "You mean, you haven't heard?" he said. "You haven't heard from Laura?"

It seemed that earlier that day Laura had telephoned my uncle and told him she'd taken up with a twenty-six-year-old man she'd met at a party. "You poor darling," my uncle said. "You're just going to have to summon all your courage now." When I kept telling Uncle Ed I couldn't believe it, he started saying things like, "Well now, I'm sure you'll be meeting other girls— you're too interesting to be left alone for long," and it was his trying to comfort me that really brought home that Laura had left me. I asked my uncle what I could do, what he would do, and he said, "Well, the fact that she hasn't told you anything might mean that she hasn't committed herself to anything yet, that she's still kind of testing the waters. But it could also mean she's just afraid to tell you because she thinks you'd go crazy. So no, I wouldn't start strategizing now or anything if I were you. I think you're just going to have to bite the bullet."

*   *   *

You could say I'd come full circle now; I was back living with my mother and back without a girlfriend. Yet one of the many ideas my uncle had lodged in my brain was that life is this continuous coming around again but always on a different plane, so that it's more a spiral than a circle. And what had put me on a very different plane now, of course, was him—my whole experience and education under him. I began to wonder, though, just how apparent my shift in planes was to my Evanston friends. They noticed, I knew, the outward change in me: the neater hair, the chino pants, the way I was always exclaiming "ex*act*ly," and the way, when they called me up on the phone and said "Keith?," I'd reply "This is he" now instead of "Yeah." One friend even noticed that whenever I talked on the phone my voice went up a key or two and became much more polished-sounding. But what my old friends couldn't know, couldn't begin to know, was the psychological gap I would sometimes feel opening up between me and them.

My friends were on my mind because now that I'd lost Laura I started seeing a lot more of them. Four of them, including David Hill and Bryan, had gone out and gotten jobs and rented an apartment together in a building right on the Evanston-Chicago border. On Saturday nights the five of us would sit around a table for hours, drinking and laughing. I'd get tipsy enough to try out some of my Uncle Ed nuggets on them— nuggets such as that according to Fran Lebowitz, the cynical New York humorist, children are a big bore because they have no fashion sense and are incapable of offering one a truly interesting *loan*. Or that, according to my uncle, even the most extreme bedroom habits need not reflect on the rest of one's life (because he knew plenty of successful New York business-women, for instance, who weren't above a little mild masochism in their sex lives, though they wouldn't dream of being subordinate to their boyfriends in any other area). And lesbians . . . "Whatever would we do without lesbians," I'd say, quoting my

uncle, "now the last remaining source of old-fashioned mascu-
line guidance?"

As I laughed my version of my uncle's deep, wicked laugh
(actually, Uncle Ed said the laugh wasn't his, for all laughs were
"borrowed" from someone else), I'd be the only one laughing.
It wasn't that my friends frowned or said anything to me, it's
what they didn't say. My remarks fell into a silence that seemed
to say, "Well, okay, whatever," as everyone quickly moved us
back to more familiar ground. Part of the problem was that it
was always so communal at their apartment. Put five young guys
together and you've got yourself a locker room, a poker party.
Bodies would slide lower into chairs as scuffed black boots were
raised and put up on the table and a big, cheap bottle of vodka
made the rounds. Then David Hill would start whapping a fresh
pack of Kools against his palm several irritating times before
finally unwrapping the cellophane and pulling out a cigarette.
My uncle said that the sad thing about straight guys is the limited emotional range they allow themselves—their scoffing un-
comfortableness with any confession of private emotion from a
fellow male means that straight guys almost always have to turn
to women to talk about their troubles.

It was so true. Because though a big, painful hole had been
blown open in me when Laura left me I never brought up how
it felt to my friends. Perhaps if I could have been alone with
Bryan, gone for a long walk with him in the night, I could have
talked about Laura to him. But every time I came over to the
apartment it was always a gang of us sitting around on Saturday
night, slugging vodka, singing songs, and joshing with each
other. Sometimes it seemed like my uncle had changed me just
enough to make me feel at home in neither Chicago nor New
York, so that I questioned my old life, my old self, yet also
wondered how legitimate any of these new aspects to me were.

I felt even more alienated from the kids at Evanston High.
My summer confidence had evaporated and been replaced by
the hungry, silent staring of the outsider. Each day at noon before heading off to my job in Wilmette I'd grab a quick lunch

at the hot dog place across from the high school. It was so tiny
it had no tables and chairs, just a wraparound counter, but what
drew me in there was the cluster of hot girls always milling
around the jukebox. As I ate my hot dog, I'd snatch glances at
the sexy, triangular creases on the crotches of their jeans, the
rips high up the back of their legs that, as they leaned over the
jukebox song menu, exposed the elastic bands of their panties.
Though these girls ignored me, had they ever engaged me in
conversation and given me the slightest encouragement, I'm
afraid my idea of entertaining small talk would have been to dust
off more of my Uncle Ed nuggets—such as that hemorrhoid
ointment applied under the eyes was the best way to get rid of
bags. Or that straight guys were actually far less rough in bed
than gay men, having been "trained" by women to be more gentle. Or that while women don't reach their sexual peak till forty,
it's all downhill for men from the age of seventeen, so that one
beautiful, forty-something New York woman who dated older
men had been heard to complain that she couldn't remember
the last time she'd had a man with more than a three-quarter
hard-on.

I began skipping the odd day of school. Nothing so regular as
what I'd done the previous year at prep school, but when I'd
wake up and see that the weather outside was my favorite kind,
a thick cloud cover lowering down, a gray quietness settling over
the morning, I'd call in sick to Evanston High, which as an
eighteen-year-old senior I could do. Then I'd set to work. Just
as years ago at the Free School I'd started writing songs on the
guitar in response to the vacuum that had suddenly opened up
around me, I now had that same urge to make something out
of the aching emptiness I felt in the wake of losing Laura and
Uncle Ed. I began writing a long short story, my first serious
piece of writing. I wanted to tell my story—from bughouse to
playing house on Fifteenth Street. I already had some confidence
I could write because my uncle had told me in our earliest days
together in New York that I had real talent; he'd even predicted

I'd go on to become "the last writer in America." And so with Handel's Concerto Grosso playing away on my mother's record player and the snow picking up speed outside the windows, I'd spend the morning writing at home. I was careful never to skip my afternoon job—if class was optional, earning money certainly wasn't.

One Sunday my uncle telephoned and after my mother spoke with him for half an hour, I got my turn with him. He told me he'd just finished his "little novel" (*Nocturnes for the King of Naples*) and, sounding excited and needy as a little child, he asked if he could read me its final pages. Suddenly I had the sense that this was his real reason for calling, that he'd endured the whole long chat with my mother just to get to this moment. It was always so flattering to feel in league with him—to feel, as he'd actually blurted out to me once in New York, "What are two exquisites like us doing in a family like this?" As my uncle began to read aloud I remembered to murmur little *mmmm*s of appreciation every few lines, though what I was hearing was such a delirious swirl of sultans and pool tables, pomegranate trees in paradise and rumbling ferryboat engines, that by the time he reached the end, with two lost dogs howling at each other through heavy fog (and through time as well?), I felt almost as lost and befogged myself. Before we hung up I read him a page or two of my own writing. Though my uncle told me when I'd finished, "I bet that's the best thing anyone wrote in Chicago today," I wondered whether he was just being generous. I myself, at least, had been disturbed by how flat my prose seemed as I read it—as though my sentences were less a worked-up piece of writing and more a bare transcript, something I might just as well have made up on the spot off the top of my head.

Not long after this telephone reading I dreamt I was with my grandmother Delilah in her high-rise apartment with its smell of mothballs and perfume. She asked me to sit with her and when I plopped down on her white sofa, it was so soft and yielding I worried I might keep sinking into it till I disappeared. Then I started worrying she'd notice that the white silk shirt I had on was not really mine, but my uncle's, the telltale sign being that the sleeves were way too long.

I had to admire how economically the dream captured all my confusion about identity. The fear of losing the self had become the fear of getting swallowed up into my grandmother's sofa; and the feeling of being an imposter who could never measure up to my uncle had been transposed into a shirt that didn't fit, that was too big for me. And as someone who'd resisted becoming Keith White, I found it appropriate that the sofa and the shirt were both white. The odd thing about the dream, though, is that it had me guiltily hoping to *conceal* from my grandmother that I was wearing my uncle's shirt, whereas in reality she and my mother were always telling me I was "just like Ed." My grandmother would even start sentences by saying "Ed—I mean, Keith . . ."

Telling kids they take after so-and-so goes on in a lot of families, I know, but in our family it was almost as though family life were a theatrical production being played out on a small stage already filled to capacity. There was no room for any new characters because all available roles had been snapped up by the original cast, so that the new generation could only serve as understudies. Thus my little brother was supposed to be just like my father, my sister like my Grandma Fleming, and I like Uncle Ed. And my stepmother, by virtue of her sneaky power behind the scenes, was held to be "another Kay"—another stepmother like Grandpa White's second wife, Kay, that is.

Though I never mentioned my shirt-and-sofa dream to my mother, I did tell her about another dream I had, one that she seemed to understand better than I. In this dream an elevator sealed itself shut on me and then rocketed me upward. When the door finally opened I was standing on the wind-raked roof of an unthinkably tall skyscraper. A team of construction workers in hard hats was busily uncoiling cables down into a large hole in the center of the building. Though I was too scared to go over there, I sensed it was an abyss whose depths extended all the way down to the ground. I thought the dream was just an illustration of my fear of heights but my mother knew immediately what it was really about: "It means you're afraid of success," she said.

When I finished my short story I mailed my uncle a copy of it. A week later I received a crisp note back from him saying that in retrospect he wished he'd been "less buddy-buddy" with me and more "dignified." He said he wouldn't be honest if he told me the story hadn't hurt him in places, "but then everyone is fair game for a writer—as I should know better than anyone since I've written about friends and family for years now without worrying too much about their feelings. No, your story is very good and you have every right to your vision of things."

I think what offended my uncle is how I had portrayed only the silly and sensational aspects of life with him. Sometimes the hardest thing for a teenage boy to write is the simple truth. And if that truth involves just how green and scared you were when you came to Uncle Ed, how you fell under his spell and how you now owed everything to him—well, it was just so much easier to write only about the come-on, the icky system, the leather bomber jacket and the cruising. I was too embarrassed to write tenderly . . . and too mannered. It can be a dangerous thing for a young writer to read *Lolita*, and not because of Humbert Humbert's thing for little girls. The Nabokov style, with its wiseass authorial presence, in my hands created a monster because I appropriated the high-handedness but not the heart.

I sent a meek note off to my uncle—not an outright apology, but close—yet weeks went by without a word from him. With a thousand miles between us, his silence took on weightiness and coldness. I found myself wondering what place, if any, I had in his life these days. For a long time there I'd felt almost like his illegitimate son, one in the tradition of Lord Chesterfield's "Dear Boy" whom Lord C. had daily worried over and guided via those brilliant letters. I remembered the day in New York when *Letters to His Son* stopped being a curiosity unrelated to me: it was the day Uncle Ed happened to mention that Chesterfield's illegitimate son "had never amounted to anything, can you believe it? All those pains for nought." Suddenly the pressure was on, I felt, not to repeat the failure. I even found pressure in my uncle's prediction that I'd become the last writer in America, since instead of seeing it as being a pretty forlorn distinction—the last idiot still scribbling away, for no one, in the age of video—I'd somehow interpreted it as meaning that I'd go on to be a lot like him as a writer.

The high point in my uncle's intensity as a father figure had been the day he suggested I change my name to Keith White. Since then, it struck me, it had been all downhill, gathering speed as I moved out of the apartment to live with Laura and then moved out of town. Now that I'd offended him with my short story, maybe he and I had reached the end of the line. For the relief I sensed in him when Laura and I went home to Chicago seemed confirmed when I happened to read an interview he'd given in which he said that artists should never have children because artists can't afford the time or the money.

It hit me that the most important person in my life was someone whose feelings for me I could never quite be sure I grasped. In my early days in New York Uncle Ed had told me once in the kitchen that he and I were in many ways alike, but so much alike that we could never feel all that comfortable in each other's presence: "You and I are like these two locomotives whose headlights are staring into each other," he'd said. This strange compliment had the effect of distancing me at the same time that it linked us together.

Perhaps the key thing I'd failed to see all along was that while he was a major character in my life, I was just a minor character in his. And now things had grown even more lopsided—now my uncle was like a star in the night sky that I could look up at and admire but never expect a response from.

All opinions needed to be revised once again after my uncle telephoned me one Sunday in December. Picking up on something in my voice, perhaps, he said, "Listen, why don't you come visit me over New Year's? Keith McDermott's off on tour with *Equus* now so I'm just here by myself." When I mentioned how puzzled I'd been at not hearing from him for so long, he said, "Oh, I know. It's terrible how out-of-sight, out-of-mind I am. Just the other day Marilyn Schaefer, my oldest friend in the world, was telling me she feels if she didn't thrust herself in front of my nose, years could go by without hearing from me."

A week later my uncle called again. He said he'd just gotten off the phone with Laura and had felt duty-bound to invite her to New York too. Laura had asked if her boyfriend, Chester, could come along but Ed held her off on that point by saying he'd have to check with me. So Chester wouldn't come, but Laura would. My uncle hoped I understood; he had his relationship with Laura too, after all. We'd all just have to make the best of it. He'd already put my plane tickets in the mail.

Instead of flying, I cashed in my tickets and took the train to New York. I couldn't see myself flying on the same plane as Laura because that would have meant having to witness her boyfriend kissing her good-bye at the airport. By the time I showed up at my uncle's apartment Laura had already been in town for hours and was now off at the Sassoon salon on Sixth Avenue getting an expensive new 'do. My uncle confided to me over glasses of chilled tap water in his kitchen that apparently Laura and Chester had barely been able to have sex these past few months. It seemed that twenty-six-year-old Chester felt so guilty about doing it with an underage girl that every time they went to bed he had a hard time getting it up. They'd had to resort to sex toys, which Laura had found sort of weird and kinky at first.

I can't remember now why Laura and I both slept on mattresses on the floor that night, her in my uncle's study, me out in the living room. Perhaps my uncle felt that to let one of us sleep in the maid's room would be to play favorites. Or maybe there were other guests at the apartment I've forgotten about. In any event, my thoughts were fixated on Laura. When she'd first swept into the apartment with a shiny, shoulder-length bob (the hairdresser had blow-dried her hair straight), she looked like a new person, a stranger I had no claim on. But when she kissed me on the lips and, brown eyes twinkling, started acting very comfortable around me, it was hard to believe that she and her familiar beauty were no longer available to me. As I lay feverishly awake that night on my mattress in the living room, I could hear that Laura was still awake in the study. Each small sound she made—turning over, little coughs—began to seem like signals sent to me. I found myself imagining, now that I knew about her bedroom frustrations with Chester, that she was feeling tempted to have sex with me. Three, four, five times or more I got up to go to the bathroom, just so I could creep down the hallway, floorboards creaking, and pass the open door of the study. A wild feeling was growing in me that Laura was on the verge of whispering to me to come join her.

But my uncle's bedroom was just across the hall from the study and what finally put an end to all my busy creeping around was the sudden cough—a very awake-, very cross-sounding cough—that issued from behind his closed door. The next morning an irritated Uncle Ed told me when we were alone in the kitchen for a moment that it was useless to try and "force anything" with Laura. I felt like snapping at him, telling him it was none of his business and, anyway, how did he know how Laura might be feeling? But I contained myself and found the stoicism he seemed to be hinting that I should be showing more of.

Soon my uncle was shooing me and Laura out of the apartment because he had some writing to do. Laura wanted to see *Saturday Night Fever*, which had just opened, so we went to a big theater on Broadway near Times Square and joined a long line snaking around the corner. The natural curliness of her hair was already creeping back into the blow-dried straightness of her new 'do, I noticed, and the image and feeling that kept haunting my mind, as the Bee Gees song "How Deep Is Your Love?" poured from some outdoor speakers, was of Laura and me out in the weather, walking the golf course fairways along the old canal. That was our time together that had touched me most deeply, I guess.

After standing in the ticket line forever, standing *on* line, as New Yorkers said, an announcement came that the show was sold out. With a couple hours to kill before meeting up with Uncle Ed at a restaurant in the Village, we loafed around Times Square and Laura remembered how I'd "really freaked" her "out" by taking her here straight from the airport when we'd flown in from Texas. What a scary introduction to New York City that had been! It was a Saturday night, she recalled, and all the whores were out standing under the beat-up doorways along Eighth Avenue. And since she and Christie had just seen the movie *Taxi Driver*, to be here in Times Square "live" now her-self—well, it was just too much. She'd worried that any minute a pimp would come bursting out of the seedy, teeming crowds to abduct her. When she'd told my uncle later where I'd taken her, he'd exclaimed, "Oh, how *stupid*! What was he thinking of?"

I had no idea she'd been so frightened by Times Square. It was way too late now for explanations, I knew, but my intention then was simply to show off to her what a hardened New Yorker I'd become. In my present dark mood it was easy to feel that maybe I'd never known how to treat Laura, how to pick up all her signals, and that someone like my uncle, who worshipped physical beauty above all else, would have been much more adept at cherishing and understanding her.

When Laura and I walked into the restaurant, Uncle Ed was already seated at a table with a ponytailed man. "This is my nephew and my . . . my friend, Laura," he said, rising to intro-duce us. But his ponytailed friend was sputtering with outrage about how Ed hadn't told him anyone else was coming to din-ner. After Ponytail had stormed out of the restaurant, Uncle Ed shrugged and told us with a sweet dimpled smile, "Oh, well; I guess misery *doesn't* always love company."

Before long I was feeling irritated with my uncle again myself. He seemed so intent on bending over backward not to favor me over Laura that he kept our conversation focused exclusively on

things that would appeal to her. After we'd talked about Laura's
Chester for a while, Uncle Ed told us he'd stopped seeing Rudy
and had taken up with this new guy, Norm.

"Is he gorgeous?" Laura asked.

"Well, he's enormous and blond. You should see what he eats
for breakfast: these slabs of strudel that he pulls out of the oven
like pizzas. But wait'll you see some of his friends, slurp, drool.
They'll all be at this party we're going to. Isn't our waiter a
dream, by the way?"

"Yeah, he is," Laura said. "Do you think he's gay?"

"Well now, darling," my uncle said, kidding her, "we've never
let that stop us before, have we?"

It really was so irritating that Laura had been invited to New
York. It had surprised me that she and Ed were even still in
contact with each other, for I'd assumed that breaking up with
me would mean she'd have to sever things with her "Teddy"
too. But my uncle could never say no to anyone, even though
he had so many people in his life that sometimes it seemed too
much for him to keep all our individual stories straight in his
mind. Just a month or so earlier, for instance, he'd been warning
me to stay away from Laura, that I "could go crazy" if I kept
brooding over her and scheming to win her back. He'd told me,
"This isn't a game, you know. It's not something you can ex-
periment with your feelings about." He'd said the only thing
that finally "cured" him of Keith McDermott was Keith's absence, his going off on tour with *Equus*.

I'd never cared much for New Year's Eve. The midnight kissing,
the fake jubilation . . . it was just all so awkward. And bringing
in the new year with Laura and my uncle's friends suddenly
seemed like something I wanted to avoid. I decided to go back
to my uncle's apartment and sulk there by myself but when I
told Laura and Ed I wasn't coming with them, they wouldn't
stop urging me to change my mind until I lied and said I was
coming down with the flu. By the time I parted with them at
the corner of Hudson and Christopher, my uncle still trying to

convince me that a hot toddy would do me good, that I could drop by for just a minute and say hi to Rudy and other friends who were always asking about me, it was twenty minutes to midnight.

There were so many things I'd never told my uncle. Since he was no longer interested, as he'd told me in Puerto Rico, in talking all night about life and love and what it all means, I'd never had the chance to tell him that I could probably spend a million years working on my self-control and still not be able to keep it cool around Laura the way he'd done for so long around Keith McDermott. And I'd never told him that while he might feel most himself in "the crossfire of a hundred eyes," I only really felt at home in marginal places: in alleyways, in the back-yard fort, on the banks of my canal. I'd never told him about those long snowy walks I used to take at the Free School and the pleasure I'd discovered in brooding. My uncle, I knew, liked his weather mild and sunny, sparkling mornings in sight of the sea where he could sit writing in his swim trunks at an umbrella table. It was his nature never to dwell on any one matter for long, to "just go skating over the surface of things," as he put it. But I'd never told him that it was my nature to linger over things, that I preferred cozily somber settings, like a humble room with windows lashed with rain, and that ever since I'd fallen under the spell of the Beatles' "This Boy" as a twelve-year-old I'd been aware that a kind of natural masochism pow-ered my most intensely lyrical feelings.

And I'd never told Uncle Ed I actually enjoyed John Updike's writing. I agreed with my uncle that Nabokov, Proust, and Tol-stoy were probably the three greatest modern writers (Nabokov for his eye, Proust for his mind, Tolstoy for his worlds). I even shared my uncle's taste for Knut Hamsun, the Norwegian nov-elist he'd told me "might be dumb but his work is so sensual and inspired." Yet while Uncle Ed dismissed Updike as "an ex-tremely intelligent man who's interested in things I'm not," I was a big fan of Updike's ordinary suburban heroes, even though it had shocked me a bit when I learned my father had always identified with Updike (I hadn't thought Dad and I had anything in common).

When the doors of the subway train opened at the Forty-second Street station, I noticed on a drab platform clock that it was exactly midnight. The station was weirdly deserted. Then I remembered that everyone was celebrating the new year somewhere aboveground. As the cold, stale breath of the station reached my face I imagined I heard a faint roar from the crowds reveling up in Times Square. The train's doors sealed shut again and I felt a brief, stabbing sense of isolation, but I didn't regret breaking away from Laura and my uncle. I didn't regret anything, really. It never occurred to me to regret having gotten mixed up with Laura—it still seemed like a miracle that she'd been attracted to me on Dr. Schwarz's psycho ward. And I had no regrets about leaving New York and Uncle Ed either. Everything that had ever happened to me seemed inevitable as fate. And everything in the future still seemed possible.